Take the Book by the Horns

Grow your business as a published expert!

Take the Book by the Horns

Grow your business as a published expert!

by Lance W. Haverkamp, and the Staff at Ghostwriter Marketing

Expert Books Publishing
Colorado Springs

Disclaimer: This publication is intended to provide helpful and informative material on
the subjects addressed. It is sold with the understanding that the publisher and author
are not engaged in providing legal, financial, or other professional services. If such
services are required, the assistance of an appropriate professional should be sought.

Although every precaution has been taken in the preparation of this book, the
publisher and author assume no responsibility for errors or omissions. Neither is any
liability assumed for damages resulting from the use of information contained herein.

The publisher and author disclaim any warranties (express or implied), merchantability,
or fitness for any particular purpose. The advice and strategies contained herein may
not be suitable for every situation. The reader should consult with a professional where
necessary.

The publisher allows content generated by artificial intelligence (AI), which is used as a
tool to expedite the creative and analytical processes of the human authors and
editors. All such use is constantly supervised, reviewed, edited, and approved by the
people involved, to ensure it meets our standards for quality and accuracy.

Title: Take the Book by the Horns: Grow your business as a published expert! / Lance
W. Haverkamp, Ghostwriter Marketing

Author: Haverkamp, Lance W. & Ghostwriter Marketing

Publication Information:
First Edition
Colorado Springs: Expert Books Publishing], 2024

Table of Contents

Unlocking the Power of a Book for Your Business

The business world is changing fast. The old playbook of cold calls, flashy ads, and one-size-fits-all messaging just doesn't cut it anymore. Today's consumers are smarter, more discerning, and frankly, overwhelmed with choices. They're not just looking for products or services; they want guidance from real experts who can help them navigate complex challenges.

This is where thought leadership comes in. It's no longer enough to just offer a great product or service. To truly stand out, you need to establish yourself as a go-to authority in your field. Building this kind of credibility is crucial for attracting high-quality clients and setting yourself apart from the competition.

But here's the catch—becoming a recognized authority isn't easy. With so many businesses clamoring for attention, how do you make your voice heard above the noise? Blog posts and networking events are fine, but they often get lost in the shuffle. To really make an impact, you need something more powerful—something that can cement your position as a leader in your industry.

Enter the book. Writing a book might sound daunting, but it's a game-changer. In the pages ahead, we'll explore how becoming an author can unlock new opportunities, draw in your ideal clients, and propel your business growth to new heights. There's something about being a published author that lends unparalleled credibility and authority. It can put you at the forefront of your field and open doors you never even knew existed.

We'll dive into strategies for leveraging your book to stand out from the crowd, build a loyal client base, and create a lasting impact in your industry. Whether you're an entrepreneur, consultant, coach, or service provider, you'll find actionable insights to guide you on this transformative journey.

So, if you're ready to take your business to the next level and embrace the new landscape of expertise, let's dive in. It's time to explore how a book can become your ultimate tool for success. Get ready to unlock your potential, differentiate yourself, and achieve the kind of growth you've always dreamed of. Your author journey starts here.

The Transformative Power of a Book

In today's cutthroat business world, standing out as an expert isn't just nice—it's necessary. Sure, there are plenty of ways to show off what you know, but let's be real: nothing quite packs the punch of authoring your own book. A well-crafted book can skyrocket your status, open doors you didn't even know existed, and leave your competition in the dust.

Think about it. When you put your ideas into a book, you're creating something tangible—something real. Blog posts come and go, videos get buried in the endless scroll, but a book? That sticks around. It's a physical testament to your knowledge and experience, something people can hold, share, and come back to again and again.

With a book, you've got the space to really dig into your subject. You can explore those complex ideas that just don't fit into a tweet or a quick video. You can lay out your thoughts, share detailed examples, and offer advice that people can actually use. This isn't just about sharing information—it's about establishing yourself as the go-to authority in your field, someone who truly gets the challenges and has the solutions.

But here's where it gets really exciting: the benefits of your book go way beyond the pages. That "published author" title? It's like a key that unlocks all sorts of doors. Suddenly, you're getting invited to speak at events, the media wants to interview you, and other big names in your industry want to collaborate. Your book becomes more than just a book—it's a powerful marketing tool that attracts clients, generates leads, and grows your business in ways you might never have imagined.

This isn't just pie-in-the-sky thinking. Countless businesses and entrepreneurs have used books to take their success to the next level. They've become recognized experts, landed high-paying clients, and scored speaking gigs that put them in front of huge audiences. The potential is real, and it's massive.

So, if you're ready to really tap into your expertise and make some noise in your crowded market, it might be time to think about writing that book. In the chapters ahead, we'll dive into real examples and strategies for using a book to launch your business into the stratosphere. Let's get started.

The Unique Challenges of Writing a Book as a Business Professional

Writing a book sounds great, but actually doing it? That's a whole different ballgame, especially when you're already juggling a busy business. It's not just about finding the time (though that's a big part of it). It's about carving out hours from your already packed schedule, often at the expense of personal time or by passing off important tasks to others. And let's be honest, for many of us, that's a tough pill to swallow.

But time isn't the only hurdle. Many business pros, even those who are rock stars in their field, start doubting themselves when it comes to putting pen to paper (or fingers to keyboard). You might know your stuff inside and out, but turning that knowledge into a compelling read? That can feel like a whole new skill set. The fear of not being able to get your ideas across in a way that really clicks with readers can be paralyzing.

Then there's the challenge of organizing all that information bouncing around in your head. You've got years of experience and insights to share, but how do you structure it all into something that makes sense? Figuring out what to include, how to present it, and in what order can feel like trying to solve a Rubik's Cube blindfolded, especially if you're not used to long-form writing.

These roadblocks can lead to a lot of frustration and self-doubt. It's no wonder many business professionals start their book with the best intentions but end up letting the project fizzle out.

But here's the thing—these challenges aren't deal-breakers. They're just obstacles, and with the right approach, support, and mindset, they're totally surmountable. You can write that book that showcases your expertise and takes your business to new heights.

One game-changing solution? Working with a skilled ghostwriter. They can take the writing load off your shoulders, letting you focus on what you do best—running your business. A good ghostwriter will help organize your ideas, structure your content, and communicate your insights in a way that really resonates with your audience. It's like having a secret weapon in your book-writing arsenal.

Remember, every author faces challenges. The key is not letting them stop you from sharing your valuable knowledge with the world.

How a Ghostwriter Can Help Overcome These Challenges

So, you get the power of a book, but the thought of actually writing one makes you break out in a cold sweat? Enter the ghostwriter—your potential secret weapon in this book-writing game.

Now, don't get the wrong idea. Working with a ghostwriter isn't about handing off your book to someone else and washing your hands of it. It's more like gaining a partner in crime—someone who can help you bring your vision to life without losing your voice in the process.

Here's the deal: a good ghostwriter will dive deep into your world. They'll pick your brain through interviews, pore over your existing content, and really get what makes you tick. The goal? To create a book that sounds unmistakably like you, even if you're not the one typing out every word.

One of the biggest perks? Time. Let's face it, as a busy professional, time is your most precious resource. With a ghostwriter, you can keep focusing on what you do best—running your business—while they handle the nitty-gritty of turning your ideas into a cohesive book. They'll do the heavy lifting of organizing your thoughts, crafting engaging prose, and making sure everything flows smoothly.

But it's not just about saving time. A skilled ghostwriter brings a whole toolkit of writing expertise to the table. They can help refine your ideas, structure your content for maximum impact, and communicate your insights in a way that really clicks with your target audience. They'll help you sidestep common pitfalls like awkward phrasing or logical leaps, ensuring your book is polished, professional, and packs a punch.

Perhaps most crucially, a good ghostwriter becomes a master of your voice. They'll tune into your unique communication style, personality, and perspective, weaving these elements throughout the book. The result? A book that truly sounds like you—authentic, credible, and trust-building.

They'll also help you nail the structure and flow of your book. They can identify your key themes, organize your ideas logically, and make sure each chapter builds on the last. They'll help you strike that sweet spot between high-level concepts and actionable advice, positioning you as an authority while delivering real value to your readers.

In essence, partnering with a ghostwriter can transform the daunting challenge of writing a book into an exciting opportunity for growth and success. It's like having a secret weapon in your arsenal—one that can help you overcome the hurdles and create a powerful tool for your business. So, if you're ready to share your expertise with the world but aren't sure where to start, a ghostwriter might just be your ticket to becoming a published author.

What You'll Get Out of This Book

Alright, if you're a business pro looking to kick things up a notch, you're in the right place. This book is your roadmap to turning a book into your secret weapon for business success. We're talking about transforming your business, becoming a go-to expert in your field, and attracting the kind of clients and deals you've always wanted.

We're going to dig deep into the power of authority. You'll see how a book can turn you into the expert everyone's looking for. It's like a turbo boost for your credibility, setting you miles apart from your competition. And get this—a book can be your ticket to speaking gigs, media spots, and partnerships you never thought possible. We're talking serious business growth potential here.

But we're not just going to tell you why you should write a book. We're going to show you how to make it work for you. You'll get battle-tested strategies for using your book to crush your business goals. Want to attract better clients? Close bigger deals? Boost your revenue? We've got you covered. You'll learn how to turn your book into a lead-generating machine and weave it into your sales process like a pro.

Now, if the idea of actually writing a book makes you break out in a cold sweat, don't worry. We're going to walk you through the whole process, including how to team up with a ghostwriter to capture your voice and expertise. Whether you're a writing newbie, or you've got a few books under your belt, you'll find what you need to create a book that truly represents your brand.

And we're not just talking theory here. We've packed this book with real-world examples and case studies of business folks who've used books to skyrocket their success. You'll get to learn from their wins (and their mistakes) so you can apply their strategies to your own business.

By the time you finish this book, you'll have a solid grasp on how a book can revolutionize your business. More importantly, you'll have the tools and know how to make it happen. Whether you're a consultant, coach, speaker, or business owner, you'll find the guidance you need to take your business to the next level.

So, if you're ready to unlock your business's full potential and establish yourself as a true industry authority, buckle up. We're about to dive into how a book can transform not just your business, but your entire professional life. Let's do this.

Who This Book is For

If you're ready to squeeze every last drop of potential out of your expertise, this book's got your name on it. Whether you're hustling as an entrepreneur, dropping wisdom as a consultant, coaching up a storm, or providing top-notch professional services, we're about to show you how a book can be your secret weapon for business growth.

Entrepreneurs, listen up. Sick of blending into the background? Tired of fighting tooth and nail for every client? We're going to show you how a book can make you stand out like a neon sign in a sea of billboards. You'll learn how to turn your book into a marketing powerhouse that attracts clients, closes deals, and fattens up your bottom line.

Consultants and coaches, this one's for you too. Want to be seen as the go-to expert in your field? We'll show you how a book can skyrocket your credibility and authority. You'll discover how to use your book to unlock new opportunities and build a business that thrives on your knowledge and experience.

And hey, all you lawyers, accountants, and financial advisors out there—we haven't forgotten about you. In your cutthroat industries, we'll show you how a book can be your golden ticket to standing out and attracting those high-quality clients you've been dreaming of.

But wait, there's more. If you're a business leader looking to put your company on the map, stick around. We'll teach you how a book can boost your brand, showcase your team's expertise, and reel in more customers than you know what to do with.

And for those of you sitting on a goldmine of knowledge but lacking the time or writing chops to get it down on paper? Don't sweat it. We'll walk you through how to team up with a ghostwriter to create a killer book that captures your voice and expertise, without eating up all your free time.

Bottom line? If you're ready to take a giant leap forward and unlock the full potential of your expertise, this book is your launchpad. Whether you're a seasoned pro or just starting out, you'll find the strategies, insights, and inspiration you need to create a book that doesn't just transform your business—it transforms your life.

So, ready to join the big leagues of business authors and thought leaders? Let's dive in and turn that book dream into a reality that crushes your goals and exceeds your wildest dreams. Game on!

What Makes This Book Different

There's no shortage of books out there claiming to help you grow your business. But this one? It's a whole different animal. We're not just rehashing the same old advice—we're bringing fresh perspectives and innovative strategies to the table that you won't find anywhere else.

Here's the deal: while other books might get bogged down in the nuts and bolts of writing and marketing, we're zooming out to look at the big picture. We're talking about the transformative power of authority—how becoming an author can fundamentally change how you're perceived in your industry and, more importantly, how it can translate into real, tangible results for your business.

And let's bust a myth right now: you don't need to be the next Shakespeare to write a book. We're pulling back the curtain on the ghostwriting process, showing you how collaboration with a pro writer can help you create a killer book without sacrificing your voice or spending every waking hour at your keyboard.

But that's just the tip of the iceberg. We've packed these pages with unconventional strategies and creative techniques that'll make you rethink everything you thought you knew about leveraging a book for business growth. We're talking outside-the-box ideas for using your book in your sales process, clever ways to repurpose your content across multiple platforms—the kind of innovative thinking that can set you miles apart from your competition.

Whether you're a seasoned author or a total newbie, get ready for some serious "aha" moments. We've got unique frameworks and exercises that'll challenge you to dig deep and think critically about your business, your audience, and your goals. And we're backing it all up with practical tips and techniques to turn your book into a growth engine on steroids.

So if you're ready to kick your business into high gear and truly unlock your potential, buckle up. This isn't just another business book—it's your roadmap to creating a book that doesn't just stand out, but blows the competition out of the water and transforms your business in ways you never thought possible.

Time to dive in and discover a whole new approach to this book-writing game. Trust us, the game-changing insights and strategies in these pages are about to rock your world. All you've got to do is turn the page and start reading. Let's do this!

Your Invitation to a Game-Changing Journey

If you're reading this, you've already taken the first step towards something big. You get it—a book isn't just a bunch of pages bound together. It's a powerhouse tool that can catapult your business to new heights. And you're ready to grab that power with both hands.

Now, let's get real for a second. This journey we're about to embark on? It's not always going to be a walk in the park. Writing a book takes guts, commitment, and a willingness to step out of your comfort zone. But trust me, the payoff? It's going to blow your mind.

When you decide to write a book, you're not just creating another product. You're making an investment—in yourself and in your business. You're planting your flag as a thought leader, setting yourself miles apart from the competition, and opening doors to opportunities you haven't even dreamed of yet. We're talking about a level of success and impact that might seem out of reach right now, but is absolutely within your grasp.

As you dive into these pages, don't just passively read. Get active. Scribble notes in the margins. Jot down ideas as they pop into your head. Start visualizing your book. What wisdom do you have locked away that the world needs to hear? What unique angle can you bring to your field? How can this book be the rocket fuel your business needs?

Remember, every epic journey starts with a single step. By picking up this book, you've already taken that step. Now it's time to keep that momentum going. Dive into these pages with an open mind, and a readiness to take action. Try out the strategies and techniques you'll learn. Start laying the groundwork for a book that's going to transform not just your business, but your entire professional life.

The potential is right there, waiting for you to seize it. All you need to do is take that next step and start writing. So, are you ready to kick off this adventure? Your book journey starts now. Let's make some magic happen!

Part 1: The Power of a Book for Establishing Authority

Chapter 1

Why a Book is the Ultimate Credibility Booster

While there are numerous strategies to boost your credibility and demonstrate your expertise, few carry the same weight and lasting impact as authoring a book. The moment you become a published author, you experience an instant authority effect that sets you apart from your peers and competitors.

When you write a book, you're not just sharing your knowledge; you're showcasing your unique perspective and experiences in a tangible, enduring format. Your book serves as a powerful testament to your expertise, providing readers with a comprehensive understanding of your insights and approaches. By articulating your ideas and methodologies clearly and compellingly, you build trust and credibility with your audience, demonstrating that you deeply understand your subject and have valuable wisdom to share.

As readers engage with your book's content, they gain a sense of your thought process, problem-solving skills, and the depth of your knowledge. By presenting well-researched, logically structured, and actionable information, you establish yourself as a reliable and authoritative source in your industry. Your book becomes a tool for building trust with potential clients, partners, and peers, as it showcases your ability to distill complex concepts into accessible, practical guidance.

Authoring a book positions you as the go-to expert in your field. When faced with a challenge or seeking advice, people naturally turn to those they perceive as authorities. By sharing your unique perspective and experiences through your book, you differentiate yourself from others in your industry and become the first point of reference when someone needs help or insights related to your area of expertise.

Your book serves as a powerful calling card, opening doors to new opportunities and elevating your professional standing. It's a tangible representation of your knowledge and skills, which can be shared, discussed, and recommended among your target audience. As more people discover and benefit from your book, your reputation as an expert grows, attracting new clients, speaking engagements, media attention, and other opportunities to showcase your expertise.

In essence, a book is the ultimate credibility booster. It establishes your authority, builds trust with your audience, and positions you as the go-to expert in your field. By investing in the creation of a high-quality, insightful book, you lay the foundation for long-term success and recognition as a true authority in your industry. Your book becomes a powerful asset that continues to work for you, attracting opportunities and cementing your reputation as a credible, knowledgeable leader in your space.

Attracting Higher-Quality Clients

When you establish yourself as an authority in your field through your book, you not only boost your credibility but also position yourself to attract higher-quality clients. These clients are typically more selective in their choice of service providers and are willing to invest in experts who have demonstrated their value and expertise.

By showcasing your knowledge and unique approach in your book, you create a powerful magnet for these discerning clients.

Having a published book sets you apart from competitors who rely solely on traditional marketing methods. It provides tangible proof of your expertise and commitment to your craft, making you a more attractive choice for clients who seek the best in their field. Your book serves as a comprehensive introduction to your philosophy, methodology, and results, allowing potential clients to gain a deep understanding of what sets you apart and how you can help them achieve their goals.

As your perceived authority grows through your book, so do client expectations, and their willingness to invest in your services. When clients view you as a true expert, they are more likely to trust your recommendations and value your time and insights. They understand that working with an authority often leads to better results, and a more seamless experience, making them more open to premium pricing and long-term engagements.

This shift in client perception can have a profound impact on your business. By attracting higher-quality clients who are eager to work with you and invest in your expertise, you can focus on projects that are more fulfilling, challenging, and financially rewarding. You'll find yourself working with clients who truly appreciate your value and are committed to implementing your strategies and recommendations, leading to greater success stories and testimonials.

Real-world examples demonstrate the power of a book in attracting better clients. For instance, a business coach who wrote a book on leadership and organizational growth found that their client base shifted from small, local businesses to Fortune 500 companies seeking their guidance. An interior designer who published a book showcasing their unique design philosophy and case studies attracted high-end residential and commercial clients who were willing to invest in their premium services.

Similarly, a marketing consultant who authored a book on innovative branding strategies saw an influx of clients from niche industries who valued their specific expertise. By sharing their knowledge and experience through their books, these professionals positioned themselves as authorities in their respective fields, attracting clients who were searching for the best and were willing to invest in their expertise.

In summary, a book is a powerful tool for attracting higher-quality clients. By establishing your authority and showcasing your unique value proposition, you position yourself to work with more selective and high-value clients who appreciate your expertise and are willing to invest in your services. As your perceived authority grows, so do client expectations and their openness to premium offerings, leading to more rewarding and impactful engagements. Real-world examples confirm that professionals who have leveraged their books to attract better clients have experienced significant growth and success in their businesses.

The "Business Card on Steroids"

First impressions are crucial. While traditional business cards have long been the standard for introducing yourself and your company, a book takes this concept to a whole new level. Often referred to as a "business card on steroids," a well-written book provides a lasting impact that far surpasses the brief exchange of contact information. When you hand someone your business card, they may glance at it briefly before tucking it away, perhaps never to be seen again. In contrast, when you give someone your book, you're offering them a tangible, value-packed resource that they can engage with on a deeper level. Your book serves as a powerful introduction to your ideas, expertise, and unique perspective, inviting the reader to explore your content and connect with your message.

Unlike a business card that merely provides surface-level information, your book allows you to showcase your knowledge, experience, and personality in a comprehensive manner. It provides an opportunity to tell your story, share your insights, and demonstrate your problem-solving abilities in a way that leaves a lasting impression on potential clients and partners.

A book serves as an excellent conversation starter. When you share your book with someone, it naturally leads to discussions about your content, your journey, and the challenges you help your clients overcome. These conversations create a more meaningful and memorable exchange than a simple business card swap, as they allow you to build rapport, establish common ground, and showcase your expertise in a relevant and engaging way.

Having a tangible, value-packed resource like a book to share with potential clients also sets you apart from competitors who rely solely on digital marketing or generic sales materials. Your book demonstrates your commitment to your craft, and your willingness to invest time and effort into creating something of value for your audience. It serves as a physical representation of your knowledge and expertise, making it a powerful leave-behind that continues to work for you long after your initial meeting.

When potential clients have your book in their hands, they have a constant reminder of your expertise, and the solutions you offer. They can refer back to your content, share it with colleagues, and use it as a resource for addressing their challenges. This ongoing exposure to your ideas and insights keeps you top-of-mind and positions you as the go-to authority in your field.

The benefits of having a book as your "business card on steroids" are clear. It provides a lasting impact, serves as a powerful introduction and conversation starter, and offers a tangible, value-packed resource that sets you apart from competitors. By leveraging your book to create meaningful connections and showcase your expertise, you can attract more high-quality clients, build stronger relationships, and establish yourself as a true authority in your industry.

In a world where business interactions are often fleeting and forgettable, a book provides a unique opportunity to make a lasting impression and create a powerful bond with potential clients. It's a marketing tool that continues to work for you long after the initial exchange, reinforcing your credibility and value with every read and shared insight.

The Media Magnet Effect

Visibility is key to establishing your authority and growing your business. While there are many strategies for attracting media attention, few are as powerful and enduring as authoring a book. When you publish a well-written, informative book, you create a media magnet that draws journalists, podcasters, and other influencers to your expertise, opening up a world of PR opportunities and increased exposure.

The media is always on the lookout for fresh perspectives, unique insights, and compelling stories. By authoring a book, you demonstrate that you have valuable knowledge to share, and a distinct point of view that sets you apart from others in your field. Your book becomes a tangible representation of your expertise, making it easier for media outlets to recognize your credibility, and the potential value you can bring to their audiences.

As your book gains traction and receives positive reviews, it can catch the attention of journalists and producers who are seeking expert sources for their stories. Your book serves as a comprehensive introduction to your ideas and experience, making it easier for media professionals to understand your expertise and how it relates to their coverage area. This can lead to invitations for interviews, guest appearances on podcasts, and quotes in articles related to your industry.

The potential for increased visibility and exposure through media coverage is immense. When you appear on a popular podcast, get featured in a major publication, or contribute to a widely-shared article, you tap into the media outlet's established audience, introducing yourself and your expertise to a vast new pool of potential clients and followers. This exposure can significantly amplify your reach and accelerate your authority-building efforts.

Media coverage lends an additional layer of credibility to your expert status. When your book and insights are featured in respected media outlets, it serves as a powerful third-party endorsement of your expertise. Potential clients and partners who may have been on the fence about working with you are more likely to view you as a trusted authority when they see that the media recognizes and values your knowledge.

As you leverage media coverage to further establish your authority, you create a virtuous cycle of increased visibility and credibility. Each media appearance or feature reinforces your expert status and attracts more opportunities for exposure. Over time, you can become a go-to source for journalists and influencers in your field, cementing your position as a thought leader and increasing your chances of being sought out for even higher-profile media engagements.

To maximize the media magnet effect of your book, it's essential to have a strategic PR plan in place. This may include crafting compelling press releases, building relationships with key media contacts, and actively pitching your expertise and book to relevant outlets. By proactively seeking out media opportunities and leveraging your book as a door-opener, you can accelerate your authority-building efforts and reach new heights of visibility and influence.

In summary, the media magnet effect of authoring a book is a powerful way to attract attention, increase your visibility, and establish your authority on a larger scale. By drawing media interest and creating opportunities for interviews, podcasts, and articles, your book can help you reach new audiences, gain third-party credibility, and cement your position as an expert in your field. With a strategic approach to leveraging media coverage, you can create a virtuous cycle of increased exposure and authority, ultimately driving more business growth and success.

Leveraging Case Studies and Examples

When it comes to establishing your authority and credibility through your book, few elements are as powerful as real-world examples and case studies. By incorporating concrete illustrations of your concepts and strategies in action, you provide readers with tangible proof of your expertise and the effectiveness of your approach. Case studies and examples serve as compelling evidence that your ideas are not just theoretical but have been successfully applied in real-world situations.

Real-world examples have a profound impact on how readers perceive and engage with your book's content. When you share stories of individuals or businesses who have implemented your strategies and achieved positive results, you create a more relatable and persuasive narrative. Readers can see themselves in these examples and envision how your insights could be applied to their own challenges and goals. This connection makes your book's concepts more memorable and actionable, increasing the likelihood that readers will trust your expertise and seek out your services.

One particularly effective way to leverage case studies is by showcasing successful books that have been used to close deals and attract clients. When you highlight how other authors in your field have used their books to generate leads, land lucrative contracts, or build their client base, you demonstrate the tangible value of a well-written book. These examples serve as powerful social proof, illustrating that authoring a book is not just a vanity project but a strategic tool for business growth.

By sharing these success stories, you inspire readers to see the potential in their own book projects. They can envision how their book could be used as a powerful marketing asset, opening doors to new opportunities and attracting ideal clients. These examples also provide valuable insights into the specific strategies and tactics that have worked for other authors, giving readers a roadmap for leveraging their own books effectively.

In addition to showcasing the success of others, it's crucial to incorporate case studies that demonstrate the effectiveness of your own approach. When you share stories of clients who have worked with you directly and achieved notable results, you provide compelling evidence of your expertise and the impact of your methods. These case studies serve as a powerful testament to your credibility and the transformative potential of your ideas.

To maximize the impact of your case studies, it's essential to present them in a clear, engaging, and relatable manner. This may involve using storytelling techniques to draw readers in, providing specific details about the challenges faced, and the strategies implemented, and highlighting the measurable results achieved. By painting a vivid picture of how your approach has been successfully applied in real-world contexts, you create a more persuasive and memorable narrative that reinforces your authority.

When selecting case studies to include in your book, aim for a diverse range of examples that showcase the breadth and versatility of your expertise. Choose stories that highlight different aspects of your approach, demonstrate your problem-solving skills, and illustrate the tangible benefits of working with you. By curating a compelling collection of case studies, you create a powerful body of evidence that supports your credibility and attracts potential clients who are seeking the results you've helped others achieve.

In summary, leveraging case studies and examples is a crucial strategy for establishing your authority and credibility through your book. By incorporating real-world illustrations of your concepts and strategies in action, showcasing successful books used for business growth, and highlighting the effectiveness of your own approach, you create a persuasive and memorable narrative that reinforces your expertise. These examples serve as powerful social proof, inspiring readers to see the potential in their own book projects and demonstrating the transformative impact of your ideas. By strategically leveraging case studies and examples throughout your book, you can create a more compelling and authoritative work that attracts ideal clients and drives business success.

Chapter 2

Positioning Your Book for Maximum Impact

One of the most critical decisions in positioning your book for maximum impact is selecting the right topic and title. Your book's core concept should encapsulate a clear and compelling message that aligns with your business goals and resonates with your target audience.

Start by identifying the key value proposition your book will offer. What unique insights, strategies or perspectives will readers gain that they can't find elsewhere? Dig deep to uncover the "hook," the most provocative and attention-grabbing angle on your area of expertise. Your topic should address your audience's most pressing pain points and desires, while establishing you as the go-to authority in your field.

As you refine your book topic, ensure it dovetails with your overall business objectives. Every element, from the subject to the tone and branding, should strategically support your company's mission, offerings and competitive positioning. Ask yourself: How will this book elevate my credibility, generate leads, and open doors to new opportunities aligned with my goals?

With a strong topic in hand, you can craft a memorable title that captures its essence and piques curiosity. Great titles are clear, specific, and evocative. They make a bold promise of value, sparking interest by hinting at the rewards within. Aim for a mix of keywords that signal your book's relevance to your audience's needs, and colorful language that lodges in the mind. Importantly, strive for a title that is unique and easy to find via search—avoiding confusion with other books is key.

Ultimately, investing time upfront to position your book's topic and title lays the foundation for its success as a business growth tool. A well-chosen concept aligns your expertise with your audience's needs and your business goals, delivered through a captivating title that stands out from the crowd. By nailing this strategic sweet spot, you'll be poised to create a book that truly maximizes its impact.

Understanding Your Target Audience

To create a book that truly resonates, you must have a deep understanding of your target audience. This goes beyond basic demographics—it's about getting inside the heads and hearts of your ideal readers, grasping their challenges, desires, and preferences on a profound level. Only then can you craft content that speaks directly to their needs and establishes a genuine connection.
Start by defining your ideal reader in vivid detail. Create an avatar that represents their key characteristics—not just age, gender, and occupation, but also their values, goals, and pain points. What keeps them up at night? What do they aspire to achieve? The more specific and nuanced your understanding, the more effectively you can tailor your book's message to strike a chord.

To gain these insights, immerse yourself in your target audience's world. Conduct market research through surveys, interviews, and focus groups to gather direct feedback. Analyze online forums, social media conversations, and book reviews in your genre to identify common themes and language patterns. Attend industry events and engage in discussions to get a pulse on the current challenges and trends affecting your readers.

As you deepen your understanding, look for ways to segment your audience based on distinct needs or preferences. While your book will have a core target reader, there may be subgroups with specific interests or concerns you can address through targeted chapters or examples. Identifying these nuances allows you to create content that is highly relevant and valuable to your entire audience.

Armed with this rich insight into your ideal reader, you can craft your book's content and messaging to resonate powerfully. Tailor your writing style and tone to match their preferences—whether that's a more formal and academic approach or a friendly and conversational voice. Use the language and terminology that naturally aligns with their world, reflecting their unique challenges and desires.

Throughout your book, aim to create a sense of dialogue with your reader. Anticipate their questions, concerns, and objections, and address them proactively. Use relatable stories and examples that mirror their experiences, creating a sense of camaraderie and trust. By demonstrating a deep understanding of their world and offering valuable solutions, you'll foster a strong connection that extends beyond the pages of your book.

Remember, understanding your target audience is an ongoing process. As you engage with readers and gather feedback, continue to refine your insights and adapt your approach. By staying attuned to their evolving needs and preferences, you'll be able to create content that consistently hits the mark and positions you as a true authority in your field.

Structuring Your Book for Engagement and Value

The structure of your book plays a crucial role in engaging readers and delivering maximum value. A well-organized, easy-to-navigate book not only enhances readability but also helps readers absorb and retain your key messages. By thoughtfully arranging your content and utilizing strategic formatting elements, you can create a compelling reading experience that keeps your audience turning the pages.

Start by creating a clear and logical flow for your book's content. Begin with an attention-grabbing introduction that establishes your core message and value proposition, setting the stage for what's to come. Then, organize your main ideas into distinct chapters, each focused on a specific theme or aspect of your topic. Within each chapter, break down complex concepts into digestible subheadings and bullet points, making it easy for readers to follow your thought process and grasp key takeaways.

As you structure your chapters, consider the natural progression of your reader's journey. Start with foundational concepts and gradually build toward more advanced ideas, creating a sense of momentum and growth. Use transitional phrases and recaps to link sections together, reinforcing key points and providing a cohesive reading experience.

To enhance engagement and readability, utilize formatting elements strategically. Incorporate descriptive subheadings that pique curiosity and provide a roadmap of what each section covers. Use bullet points and numbered lists to highlight important ideas and break up dense passages of text. Employ visual elements like charts, graphs, and illustrations to reinforce key concepts and provide a visual break from long blocks of text.

In addition to structural elements, consider incorporating interactive features that actively engage readers and provide practical value. Include thought-provoking questions or prompts that encourage readers to reflect on their own experiences and apply your insights to their unique situations. Offer exercises or worksheets that guide readers through a step-by-step process, helping them put your ideas into action. By making your book an interactive experience, you'll not only deepen reader engagement but also increase the likelihood that they'll recommend your book to others.

As you craft your book's structure, keep your target audience's preferences and needs at the forefront. Consider the format that will best serve your readers, whether that's short, punchy chapters ideal for busy professionals or longer, more in-depth explorations suited for a more academic audience. Solicit feedback from beta readers, or a focus group to gauge the effectiveness of your structure and make adjustments as needed.

Ultimately, a well-structured book is a powerful tool for engaging readers and delivering lasting value. By creating a clear, logical flow, utilizing strategic formatting elements, and incorporating interactive features, you'll craft a reading experience that not only informs and inspires but also positions you as a trusted authority in your field. So take the time to thoughtfully organize your content, and watch as your book becomes a go-to resource that readers return to time and again.

The Power of Storytelling in Nonfiction

While nonfiction books aim to inform and educate, the most impactful ones also engage readers on a deeper, emotional level. This is where storytelling comes in. By weaving compelling stories and anecdotes throughout your book, you can create a powerful connection with your audience, making your ideas more memorable and inspiring readers to take action.

At its core, storytelling taps into the fundamental human craving for narrative. We are wired to respond to stories, which have been used for centuries to pass down knowledge, share experiences, and convey important lessons. In the context of your nonfiction book, stories serve to illustrate your key points, making abstract concepts tangible and relatable. They engage readers' emotions, sparking empathy, curiosity, and motivation.

To harness the power of storytelling in your book, start by identifying the core themes and messages you want to convey. Then, brainstorm relevant stories and anecdotes that exemplify these ideas. These can be drawn from your own experiences, case studies of clients or customers, or even historical events and figures. The key is to choose stories that are both engaging and illustrative, with clear ties to your main points.

When crafting your stories, employ techniques that draw readers in and keep them hooked. Start with a compelling hook that piques curiosity and sets the stage for the narrative. Use vivid, sensory language to create a rich, immersive experience, transporting readers into the scene. Develop relatable characters and dialogue that bring the story to life, making it easy for readers to connect with the people and situations described.

As you weave stories into your book, be strategic about their placement and pacing. Use them to punctuate key insights, providing a momentary break from denser informational content. Vary the length and style of your stories to maintain reader interest, alternating between brief anecdotes and more extended narratives. Importantly, ensure that each story serves a clear purpose, advancing your argument or illustrating a specific point.

While storytelling is a powerful tool, it's important to strike a balance between narrative and practical advice. Remember that readers turn to nonfiction books primarily for information and guidance, so your stories should complement and enhance your core content, not overwhelm it. Use stories as a means to reinforce your ideas, but always circle back to the key takeaways and actionable insights readers can apply to their own lives.

One effective way to balance storytelling with information is to follow a "story-lesson-application" structure. Begin with an engaging anecdote that captures readers' attention and emotions. Then, extract the key lessons or insights from the story, explaining how they relate to your broader themes. Finally, provide concrete examples or steps readers can take to apply these lessons in their own contexts, bridging the gap between narrative and practical value.

By harnessing the power of storytelling in your nonfiction book, you can create a richer, more engaging reading experience that resonates with readers on multiple levels. Your stories will not only make your ideas more memorable and impactful but also forge a deeper connection with your audience, inspiring them to embrace your message and take action. So as you craft your book, remember to weave in compelling stories that educate, inspire, and transform, making your nonfiction work a powerful tool for change.

The Credibility Boost of Testimonials and Forewords

Readers need to trust that your ideas are reliable, your insights are valid, and your expertise is genuine. One powerful way to establish this trust is through the use of testimonials and forewords from respected figures in your industry. By leveraging the power of social proof, you can significantly boost your book's credibility and attract a wider audience.

At its core, social proof is the idea that we look to others to guide our own beliefs and behaviors. When we see respected individuals endorsing a product, service, or idea, we're more likely to view it as trustworthy and valuable. In the context of your book, testimonials and forewords serve as potent forms of social proof, signaling to readers that your work has been vetted and approved by experts they admire.

To harness this credibility boost, start by identifying key figures in your industry whose endorsement would carry significant weight. These may be thought leaders, influencers, or professionals with a strong track record of success. Consider individuals whose values and perspectives align with your own, and whose audiences overlap with your target readership.

When reaching out to potential testimonial writers, craft a compelling request that highlights the value of your book and the benefits of being associated with it. Share a brief synopsis of your key ideas and explain how their endorsement would help spread your message to a wider audience. Be specific about what you're asking for whether it's a short blurb, or a more extended testimonial, and provide clear guidelines for format and length.

As you gather testimonials, aim for diversity in terms of perspective and expertise. A mix of endorsements from established thought leaders, up-and-coming influencers, and satisfied clients or readers will paint a well-rounded picture of your book's value. Be sure to showcase these testimonials strategically, placing them on your book's cover, in the front matter, and throughout your promotional materials.

In addition to testimonials, consider securing a foreword from a well-known expert or influencer in your field. A foreword is a short introduction to your book, typically written by someone other than the author, that lends credibility and context to your work. By having a respected figure vouch for your ideas and expertise, you can significantly boost your book's authority and appeal.

When choosing a foreword writer, look for someone whose name and reputation will instantly catch readers' attention. Ideally, this should be a person whose endorsement would be seen as a major coup, signaling that your book is a must-read in your industry. Approach potential foreword writers with a personalized request that demonstrates your familiarity with their work and explains why their endorsement would be particularly meaningful.

As with testimonials, be specific about what you're asking for in a foreword. Provide a clear brief that outlines your book's key themes, target audience, and desired tone. Be open to feedback and suggestions from your foreword writer, as their unique perspective can add depth and nuance to your book's introduction.

By leveraging the credibility boost of testimonials and forewords, you can significantly enhance your book's authority and appeal. These endorsements serve as powerful forms of social proof, signaling to readers that your ideas have been vetted and approved by respected experts in your field. So as you craft your book, don't overlook the value of these credibility-enhancing tools. Seek out endorsements from key figures, showcase them strategically, and watch as your book gains traction and influence in your industry.

Creating a Strong Author Bio and "About the Author" Section

In the world of nonfiction books, your credibility as an author is just as important as the ideas you present. Readers want to know that they're learning from someone with genuine expertise, and a track record of success in their field. This is where a strong author bio and "About the Author" section come into play. By crafting compelling descriptions of your background and achievements, you can establish yourself as a trusted authority and build rapport with your audience.

Your author bio is a short, snappy introduction to who you are and what you bring to the table. It should be concise, yet powerful, painting a picture of your unique qualifications and perspective. To create a bio that packs a punch, start by highlighting your most impressive achievements and credentials. This might include your professional titles, notable clients or projects, published works, or media appearances.

When deciding what to include, think about the elements of your background that are most relevant to your book's subject and target audience. If you're writing about leadership, for example, you might emphasize your experience as a CEO or executive coach. If your book focuses on personal development, you might highlight your work as a therapist or your own journey of growth and transformation.

In addition to your achievements, your author bio should convey a sense of your personality and values. Use language that reflects your unique voice and perspective, and don't be afraid to inject some humor or vulnerability. The goal is to come across as relatable and authentic, while still maintaining a sense of authority and professionalism.

Once you've crafted your author bio, leverage it across all your promotional materials, from your book cover and website to your social media profiles and speaking engagements. Consistency is key here— by presenting a unified brand and message, you'll reinforce your credibility and make a lasting impression on potential readers.

In addition to your short bio, consider including a more detailed "About the Author" section in your book's back matter. This is your opportunity to dive deeper into your background, qualifications, and personal story. Use this space to elaborate on the experiences and insights that have shaped your perspective and expertise.

In your "About the Author" section, you might include details about your education, career trajectory, and key milestones or turning points. You can also share anecdotes or stories that illustrate your passion for your subject matter and your commitment to your readers' success. By giving readers a behind-the-scenes look at your journey, you'll create a sense of connection and trust that can last well beyond the pages of your book.

When crafting your "About the Author" section, keep in mind the same principles that guide your shorter bio. Use language that is engaging, authentic, and reflective of your unique voice. Be selective in what you include, focusing on the elements of your background that are most relevant and compelling to your target audience. And don't be afraid to let your personality shine through—after all, your readers are investing not just in your ideas, but in you as an individual.

By creating a strong author bio and "About the Author" section, you can establish yourself as a credible, trustworthy authority in your field. These elements of your book serve as powerful tools for building rapport with readers and reinforcing the value of your ideas. So take the time to craft descriptions that showcase your expertise, achievements, and unique perspective—and watch as your audience grows, and your influence expands.

Designing a Professional Book Cover and Interior Layout

In the world of publishing, the old adage "don't judge a book by its cover" is often ignored. The reality is that readers do judge books by their covers, and by their interior design as well. A visually appealing, professional book design is essential for capturing attention, conveying your book's value, and creating a positive reading experience. By investing in high-quality cover design and interior layout, you can ensure that your book stands out on the shelf and makes a lasting impression on your audience.

Let's start with your book cover. This is your first and best chance to grab potential readers' attention and persuade them to pick up your book. A great cover design should be eye-catching, memorable, and reflective of your book's core themes and tone. It should also be professionally designed, with high-quality graphics and typography that convey a sense of credibility and value.

When designing your book cover, there are several key elements to consider. First and foremost is typography. Your book's title and subtitle should be clearly legible and visually appealing, with a font choice that reflects your book's genre and tone. Opt for clean, easy-to-read fonts that don't distract from your message, and use font size and placement to create a clear visual hierarchy.

Imagery is another crucial element of effective book cover design. Choose graphics or photographs that are high-quality, relevant to your book's themes, and emotionally resonant with your target audience. If you're using illustrations or custom graphics, ensure that they are professionally designed and align with your overall brand and aesthetic.

Color is also a powerful tool in book cover design. Different colors evoke different emotions and associations, so pick a color scheme that aligns with your book's tone and message. Bold, bright colors can convey energy and excitement, while more muted tones can suggest sophistication and authority. Consider using color to create contrast and draw the eye to key elements of your design.

Once you've captured readers' attention with your cover, it's crucial to maintain a professional, engaging experience throughout the interior of your book. Your interior layout should be clean, easy to navigate, and visually appealing, with thoughtful choices around font, margins, and white space.

When choosing fonts for your book's interior, prioritize readability above all else. Opt for classic, easy-to-read fonts like Arial, Helvetica, or Garamond, and use a font size that is comfortable for extended reading (typically 10-12 points). Avoid using too many fonts or font sizes, as this can create visual clutter and distract from your content.

Margins and white space are also key considerations in interior layout. Generous margins not only create a more visually appealing page but also make your book easier to hold and navigate. Use white space strategically to break up dense passages of text and create a sense of balance and flow. Consider using elements like pull quotes, subheadings, and bullet points to further enhance readability and engagement.

Finally, pay attention to small details like page numbers, chapter titles, and section breaks. These elements should be consistent throughout your book and reflect your overall design aesthetic. Use high-quality paper stock and printing techniques to ensure that your book feels professional and substantial in the reader's hands.

By designing a professional book cover and interior layout, you can create a reading experience that is both visually appealing and intellectually engaging. A well-designed book conveys a sense of credibility, authority, and value, and can help you stand out in a crowded marketplace. So don't skimp on design—invest in high-quality cover and interior design that reflects your unique brand and message, and watch as your book makes a lasting impression on readers.

Chapter 3

Unlocking the Power of Ghostwriting

Many business professionals harbor the misconception that to establish their authority and credibility, they must write their book entirely on their own. This belief often stems from the notion that true authorship requires a mastery of writing skills, and a natural flair for putting words on paper. However, the reality is that countless successful books, including those in the business world, have been created with the help of ghostwriters.

Ghostwriting is a prevalent practice in the publishing industry, where skilled writers collaborate with subject-matter experts to craft compelling and informative books. These professional writers possess the ability to transform ideas, insights, and experiences into well-structured, engaging content that resonates with readers. By partnering with a ghostwriter, business professionals can focus on their area of expertise, and the valuable knowledge they wish to share, rather than getting bogged down in the intricacies of the writing process.

It's essential to recognize that the true value of a book lies in its content, not in the mechanics of its creation. Your unique perspective, hard-won lessons, and innovative strategies are what will establish your authority and provide immense value to your readers. The role of a ghostwriter is to help you articulate your ideas and present them in a compelling manner, ensuring that your book effectively communicates your message and resonates with your target audience.

Embracing the concept of ghostwriting allows you to prioritize your core competencies and allocate your time and energy where they are most impactful. By collaborating with a skilled writer, you can streamline the book creation process and bring your vision to life more efficiently, without compromising on quality or authenticity.

Throughout this chapter, we will explore the many benefits of working with a ghostwriter and how this collaborative approach can help you unlock the power of your expertise and transform it into a valuable resource for your business growth. We encourage you to shift your focus from the perceived challenges of writing to the immense potential of your ideas, and the impact they can have on your audience. Embracing the support of a ghostwriter is not a shortcut, but rather a strategic decision that can amplify your message and accelerate your journey to becoming a published authority in your field.

What a Ghostwriter Does

A ghostwriter is a professional writer who collaborates with subject-matter experts, such as business professionals, to create a book that reflects the expert's knowledge, experiences, and unique voice. The ghostwriter's primary role is to transform the expert's ideas and insights into a well-structured, compelling, and polished manuscript that effectively communicates their message to the target audience.

The ghostwriting process is highly collaborative, requiring a close partnership between the expert and the writer. This collaboration begins with the ideation phase, where the ghostwriter works with the expert to define the book's central theme, target audience, and desired outcomes. Through in-depth interviews and discussions, the ghostwriter gains a deep understanding of the expert's knowledge, experiences, and unique perspectives, which form the foundation of the book's content.

Once the book's direction and structure are established, the ghostwriter begins the process of organizing and developing the content. This involves breaking down complex ideas into easily digestible sections, crafting engaging narratives, and ensuring a logical flow throughout the book. The ghostwriter's skill lies in their ability to capture the expert's voice and style, creating a manuscript that authentically represents the expert's thoughts and personality.

Throughout the writing process, the ghostwriter, and expert maintain open communication and feedback loops. The ghostwriter shares drafts and chapters with the expert for review, allowing them to provide input, clarify ideas, and ensure the content accurately reflects their vision. This iterative process of writing, reviewing, and refining continues until both parties are satisfied with the final manuscript.

In addition to the actual writing, a ghostwriter also plays a crucial role in the editing and polishing stages. They meticulously revise the manuscript, ensuring clarity, coherence, and grammatical accuracy. The ghostwriter's editorial expertise helps elevate the book's quality, making it a professional and impactful resource that resonates with readers.

The key stages of working with a ghostwriter can be summarized as follows:

1. Ideation and planning: Defining the book's theme, audience, and structure.
2. Research and content gathering: Conducting interviews and collecting relevant information.
3. Writing and development: Crafting the manuscript based on the expert's insights and feedback.
4. Editing and polishing: Refining the manuscript for clarity, coherence, and impact.

5. Final review and approval: Ensuring the expert is satisfied with the completed book.

By understanding the role and responsibilities of a ghostwriter, business professionals can appreciate the value of this collaborative approach to book creation. A skilled ghostwriter brings expertise in writing, editing, and project management, allowing the expert to focus on their core competencies while still producing a high-quality book that establishes their authority and supports their business growth.

The Benefits of Working with a Ghostwriter

Collaborating with a skilled ghostwriter offers numerous advantages for business professionals seeking to create a high-quality book that captures their unique voice and expertise. By partnering with a ghostwriter, you can effectively articulate your ideas, structure your content, and save valuable time throughout the book creation process.

Capturing Your Unique Voice and Expertise: One of the primary benefits of working with a ghostwriter is their ability to capture your unique voice and expertise. Through in-depth interviews and discussions, a ghostwriter gains a deep understanding of your knowledge, experiences, and perspectives. They use this understanding to craft a narrative that authentically represents your ideas and insights, ensuring that the book truly reflects your voice and style.

Ghostwriters employ various techniques to capture your unique voice, such as:

- Active listening and probing questions to draw out your most valuable insights
- Studying your existing content, such as blog posts or presentations, to understand your communication style
- Collaborating with you to develop a consistent tone and style throughout the book

- Incorporating your feedback and revisions to ensure the content accurately represents your thoughts and ideas

By leveraging these techniques, a ghostwriter ensures that the final manuscript is a genuine reflection of your expertise, allowing your unique voice to shine through and connect with your target audience.

The Collaborative Process and Bringing Structure to Your Content: Another significant benefit of working with a ghostwriter is their experience in organizing and structuring book content. Ghostwriters are skilled at taking complex ideas and transforming them into a clear, logical, and engaging narrative. They understand how to break down your expertise into digestible sections, create smooth transitions between chapters, and maintain a coherent flow throughout the book.

The collaborative process between you and your ghostwriter is essential to achieving a well-structured and impactful book. Effective collaboration involves:

- Regular communication and feedback sessions to ensure alignment and address any concerns
- Iterative reviews of drafts and chapters to refine the content and structure
- Flexibility and adaptability to incorporate your insights and preferences into the manuscript
- Establishing clear expectations and timelines to keep the project on track

By fostering a strong collaborative relationship with your ghostwriter, you can leverage their experience and expertise to create a book that is well-organized, engaging, and effectively communicates your message to your target audience.

Time-Saving Advantages: Perhaps one of the most significant benefits of working with a ghostwriter is the time-saving advantage it offers. As a business professional, your time is valuable, and writing a book from scratch can be a time-consuming and daunting task. By partnering with a ghostwriter, you can focus on your core business activities and areas of expertise while still producing a high-quality book that supports your goals.

When you collaborate with a ghostwriter, you benefit from:

- Dedicated writing time without detracting from your primary responsibilities
- Efficient content creation, as the ghostwriter handles the heavy lifting of the writing process
- Streamlined project management, with the ghostwriter keeping the book on track and adhering to timelines
- More time to focus on your business growth, client relationships, and other strategic initiatives

By leveraging the expertise and efficiency of a ghostwriter, you can create a valuable book asset for your business without sacrificing your time or compromising on quality.

In summary, working with a ghostwriter offers numerous benefits, including capturing your unique voice and expertise, bringing structure and clarity to your content, and saving you valuable time throughout the book creation process. By collaborating with a skilled ghostwriter, you can create a powerful tool that establishes your authority, enhances your credibility, and supports your business growth objectives.

The Importance of Clear Communication and Setting Expectations

When embarking on a ghostwriting collaboration, clear communication and setting expectations are paramount to ensuring a successful outcome. Open and transparent communication between the author and ghostwriter lays the foundation for a productive partnership, while establishing clear expectations and boundaries helps maintain a smooth and efficient working relationship.

Discussing the Significance of Open and Transparent Communication: Open and transparent communication is essential to fostering a strong collaboration between the author and ghostwriter. From the initial consultation to the final manuscript review, both parties must feel comfortable sharing ideas, providing feedback, and addressing concerns. Regular, honest communication helps ensure that the book remains aligned with the author's vision and expertly captures their unique voice and expertise.

Key aspects of open and transparent communication include:

- Scheduling regular check-ins and progress updates to maintain alignment and address any issues promptly
- Encouraging the author to provide candid feedback on drafts and revisions to ensure their satisfaction with the content
- Being transparent about challenges, limitations, or changes in direction to maintain trust and accountability
- Celebrating milestones and successes together to foster a positive and supportive working relationship

By prioritizing open and transparent communication, authors and ghostwriters can build a strong foundation of trust and collaboration, leading to a more effective and enjoyable book creation process.

Establishing Clear Expectations and Boundaries: Setting clear expectations and boundaries from the outset is crucial to ensuring a successful ghostwriting collaboration. By defining the scope of work, deadlines, revisions, and feedback processes upfront, both the author and ghostwriter can work together efficiently and avoid misunderstandings or delays.

Important expectations and boundaries to establish include:

- Project scope and deliverables, including word count, number of chapters, and any additional materials (e.g., foreword, author bio)
- Timeline for completion, with specific milestones and deadlines for drafts, revisions, and final manuscript submission

- Revision and feedback processes, including the number of rounds of revisions included, and the expected turnaround time for each round
- Communication preferences, such as the frequency of check-ins, preferred methods of communication (e.g., email, phone, video conferencing), and any "off-limits" times
- Confidentiality and non-disclosure agreements to protect the author's intellectual property and sensitive information

By clearly defining these expectations and boundaries, authors and ghostwriters can work together more effectively, minimize the risk of misunderstandings, and ensure a smooth and successful collaboration.

Ensuring a Shared Understanding of the Book's Purpose, Tone, and Style: Before diving into the writing process, it is essential for the author and ghostwriter to have a shared understanding of the book's purpose, tone, and style. This alignment helps ensure that the final manuscript effectively communicates the author's message and resonates with their target audience.

To achieve this shared understanding, authors and ghostwriters should:

- Discuss the book's central theme, key takeaways, and desired impact on the reader
- Define the target audience and their preferences, challenges, and expectations
- Agree on the book's overall tone and style, such as formal or conversational, humorous or serious, or storytelling versus instructional
- Review examples of the author's existing content or preferred writing styles to ensure consistency and authenticity
- Create a detailed outline or content plan that reflects the agreed-upon purpose, tone, and style

By ensuring a shared understanding of these essential elements from the outset, authors and ghostwriters can work together more harmoniously and create a book that effectively achieves its intended purpose and resonates with the target audience.

In summary, clear communication and setting expectations are vital components of a successful ghostwriting collaboration. By fostering open and transparent communication, establishing clear expectations and boundaries, and ensuring a shared understanding of the book's purpose, tone, and style, authors and ghostwriters can build a strong partnership that results in a high-quality, impactful book that achieves the author's goals and supports their business growth.

The Importance of Book Quality and Professionalism

In the world of business books, quality and professionalism are essential factors that can make or break an author's success. A well-written, professionally edited book has the power to enhance your credibility and authority, while a poorly written or amateurish book can have detrimental effects on your reputation and brand. Understanding the importance of book quality and professionalism is crucial when collaborating with a ghostwriter to ensure that your final product is polished, impactful, and reflects your expertise in the best possible light.

The Impact of a Well-Written, Professionally Edited Book: A high-quality book that is well-written and professionally edited can significantly enhance your credibility and authority within your industry. When your book is crafted with care, expertise, and attention to detail, it demonstrates your commitment to excellence and reinforces your position as a thought leader in your field.

Professional editing and proofreading play a crucial role in ensuring a polished final product. A professional editor can help refine your book's structure, clarity, and flow, while a proofreader meticulously reviews the manuscript for grammar, punctuation, and formatting errors. By investing in these essential services, you can be confident that your book will make a positive and lasting impression on your readers, reinforcing your credibility and authority as an expert in your domain.

Pitfalls of Poorly Written or Amateurish Books: On the other hand, a poorly written or amateurish book can have severe negative consequences for your reputation and brand. A subpar book can undermine your credibility, causing readers to question your expertise and the value of your insights. In today's competitive market, where readers have countless options, a book that fails to meet professional standards can quickly tarnish your hard-earned reputation and hinder your business growth efforts.

When working with a ghostwriter, it's essential to be aware of common mistakes and red flags that can compromise the quality of your book. These may include:

- Lack of experience or expertise in your specific industry or subject
- Poor communication or responsiveness throughout the writing process
- Failure to capture your unique voice and style authentically
- Missed deadlines or a lack of professionalism in meeting commitments
- Subpar writing quality or a lack of attention to detail in the drafts and revisions

By being vigilant and proactive in addressing these potential pitfalls, you can protect your reputation and ensure that your book meets the highest standards of quality and professionalism.

The Role of a Ghostwriter in Ensuring a High-Quality Final Product: A skilled and experienced ghostwriter plays a vital role in ensuring that your book is of the highest quality. A ghostwriter's primary responsibility is to deliver a well-crafted and engaging manuscript that effectively communicates your ideas, insights, and expertise to your target audience.

To achieve this, a ghostwriter must:

- Possess strong writing skills, and the ability to adapt to your unique voice and style
- Have a deep understanding of your industry and subject to ensure accuracy and relevance
- Structure the book in a logical and compelling manner that keeps readers engaged
- Collaborate closely with you throughout the writing process to ensure alignment with your vision and goals
- Be receptive to feedback and willing to make revisions to refine the manuscript

Open communication and feedback are essential throughout the writing process to ensure that the final product meets your expectations and adheres to the highest standards of quality. By maintaining a transparent and collaborative relationship with your ghostwriter, you can work together to create a book that showcases your expertise, engages your readers, and supports your business growth objectives.

Book quality, and professionalism aren't optional. A well-written, professionally edited book has the power to elevate your credibility and authority, while a poorly executed book can have damaging effects on your reputation and brand. By partnering with a skilled ghostwriter who is committed to delivering a high-quality final product and maintaining open communication and feedback throughout the process, you can ensure that your book is a powerful tool for establishing your expertise and driving your business success.

Ensuring Confidentiality and Discretion

When collaborating with a ghostwriter, confidentiality and discretion are of utmost importance. As an author, you will be sharing sensitive information, proprietary ideas, and personal experiences throughout the writing process. It is crucial to work with a ghostwriter who understands the significance of confidentiality and has measures in place to protect your information and intellectual property.

The Importance of Confidentiality in the Ghostwriting Relationship: Confidentiality forms the foundation of a successful ghostwriting relationship. When you share your ideas, knowledge, and experiences with your ghostwriter, you are entrusting them with valuable and often sensitive information. A professional ghostwriter understands the importance of safeguarding this information and maintaining the highest levels of confidentiality throughout the collaboration and beyond.

Confidentiality in ghostwriting extends beyond just protecting your personal information; it also includes preserving your intellectual property rights. Your book's content, including your unique ideas, strategies, and insights, is your intellectual property. A ghostwriter who values confidentiality will take steps to ensure that your intellectual property is protected and that your book's content remains confidential until you are ready to publish.

Best Practices for Protecting Sensitive Information and Ideas: To ensure that your sensitive information and ideas are protected during the ghostwriting process, it is essential to follow best practices for confidentiality. These practices include:

1. Secure communication channels: Use secure, encrypted communication methods such as password-protected email or secure file-sharing platforms to exchange sensitive information and drafts.
2. Limited access to materials: Ensure that only necessary parties, such as the ghostwriter and editor, have access to your book's content during the writing and editing process.
3. Secure storage of files: Your ghostwriter should store all files and documents related to your book on secure, encrypted devices or cloud storage services.
4. Confidentiality training for team members: If your ghostwriter works with a team, ensure that all team members are trained in confidentiality best practices and have signed appropriate agreements.

5. Discreet communication: Your ghostwriter should be discreet when discussing your project, avoiding sharing details or mentioning your name in public settings or with unauthorized parties.

By adhering to these best practices, you and your ghostwriter can create a secure and confidential environment that protects your sensitive information and ideas throughout the book creation process.

Establishing Clear Confidentiality Agreements and Contracts: To further protect your confidentiality and intellectual property rights, it is essential to establish clear confidentiality agreements and contracts with your ghostwriter. These legal documents outline the terms and conditions of your collaboration, including confidentiality clauses and intellectual property ownership.

A well-drafted confidentiality agreement should include:

1. Definition of confidential information: Clearly outline what constitutes confidential information in your collaboration, such as your ideas, strategies, personal experiences, and drafts.
2. Obligations of the ghostwriter: Specify the ghostwriter's responsibilities in protecting your confidential information, including non-disclosure and secure handling of materials.
3. Duration of confidentiality: Establish the time frame for which the confidentiality agreement remains in effect, which may extend beyond the completion of the book project.
4. Consequences of breach: Outline the legal consequences and remedies available in case of a breach of confidentiality by the ghostwriter.

In addition to a confidentiality agreement, your contract with the ghostwriter should clearly define the ownership of the book's intellectual property rights. Ensure that the contract specifies that you, as the author, retain all rights to the book's content and that the ghostwriter's role is to assist in the creation of the work on a work-for-hire basis.

By establishing clear confidentiality agreements and contracts, you can protect your sensitive information and intellectual property rights, ensuring a secure and successful ghostwriting collaboration.

In summary, confidentiality, and discretion are crucial aspects of a professional ghostwriting relationship. By working with a ghostwriter who understands the importance of confidentiality, follows best practices for protecting sensitive information, and enters into clear confidentiality agreements and contracts, you can collaborate with peace of mind, knowing that your ideas and intellectual property are secure. This foundation of trust and confidentiality allows you to focus on creating a high-quality book that showcases your expertise and supports your business growth.

The Cost-Benefit Analysis

Investing in ghostwriting services is a significant decision that requires careful consideration of various factors, including the upfront costs and the potential long-term return on investment (ROI) for your business and brand. By understanding the cost-benefit analysis of working with a ghostwriter, you can make an informed decision and develop strategies to maximize the value and impact of your book investment.

Factors to Consider When Weighing the Investment in Ghostwriting Services: When evaluating the investment in ghostwriting services, it's essential to consider several key factors:

1. Time savings: Working with a ghostwriter allows you to leverage their expertise and efficiency, saving you valuable time that you can dedicate to your core business activities and revenue-generating pursuits.
2. Opportunity costs: Consider the potential opportunities you may miss out on if you were to write the book yourself, such as focusing on client acquisition, product development, or strategic partnerships.

3. Quality and professionalism: A professionally written book by an experienced ghostwriter can significantly enhance the quality and impact of your book, leading to better reception and results compared to a self-written book.
4. Market positioning: Assess how a high-quality book can help you stand out in your industry, establish your authority, and attract your ideal clients or customers.
5. Long-term value: Evaluate the potential long-term benefits of having a well-written book, such as generating leads, securing speaking engagements, and creating new revenue streams.

By carefully weighing these factors against the upfront costs of ghostwriting services, you can make a well-informed decision that aligns with your business goals and resources.

The Long-Term ROI of a Professionally Written Book: While the upfront investment in ghostwriting services may seem substantial, it's crucial to consider the long-term ROI of a professionally written book for your business and brand. A high-quality book can serve as a powerful marketing tool, helping you:

1. Establish your authority and credibility: A well-written book positions you as an expert in your field, increasing your credibility and trust among your target audience.
2. Attract ideal clients and customers: By showcasing your expertise and unique insights, your book can help you attract higher-quality leads and clients who value your knowledge and services.
3. Generate passive income: A professionally written book can create new revenue streams through book sales, affiliate marketing, and other related products or services.
4. Secure media and speaking opportunities: A compelling book can open doors to media interviews, podcasts, and speaking engagements, providing additional exposure and credibility for your brand.

5. Build a loyal following: By providing valuable insights and solutions to your readers, your book can help you build a loyal following of engaged fans and advocates who support your business.

When considering the long-term ROI, it becomes clear that investing in a professionally written book can yield significant returns for your business and brand, far outweighing the initial costs of ghostwriting services.

Strategies for Maximizing the Value and Impact of Your Book Investment: To ensure that you maximize the value and impact of your book investment, consider implementing the following strategies:

1. Develop a comprehensive book marketing plan: Create a detailed plan for promoting your book through various channels, such as social media, email marketing, and paid advertising, to reach your target audience effectively.
2. Leverage your book for lead generation: Use your book as a lead magnet to attract potential clients or customers, offering a free chapter or bonus resources in exchange for their contact information.
3. Integrate your book into your business strategy: Incorporate your book into your overall business strategy, using it as a tool for client onboarding, employee training, or thought leadership positioning.
4. Seek strategic partnerships and collaborations: Identify potential partners or collaborators who can help expand your book's reach and impact, such as industry influencers, complementary businesses, or professional associations.
5. Repurpose your book content: Maximize the value of your book's content by repurposing it into various formats, such as blog posts, podcasts, webinars, or online courses, to reach a wider audience and create additional revenue streams.

By implementing these strategies, you can amplify the impact and ROI of your professionally written book, ensuring that your investment in ghostwriting services pays dividends for years to come.

Conducting a thorough cost-benefit analysis is essential when considering investing in ghostwriting services. By evaluating factors such as time savings, opportunity costs, and long-term ROI, you can make an informed decision that aligns with your business goals and resources. Moreover, by implementing strategies to maximize the value and impact of your book investment, you can leverage your professionally written book to establish your authority, attract ideal clients, and create new growth opportunities for your business and brand.

Part 2: Leveraging Your Book for Business Growth

Chapter 4

The Psychology of Reciprocity

Reciprocity is a fundamental concept in human behavior that has been observed and studied across various disciplines, including psychology, sociology, and anthropology. At its core, reciprocity refers to the social norm of responding to a positive action with another positive action. In other words, when someone does something nice for us, we feel compelled to return the favor.

The principle of reciprocity is deeply ingrained in human nature and has evolutionary roots. From an evolutionary perspective, reciprocity has played a crucial role in the survival and thriving of human societies. Our ancestors lived in close-knit communities where cooperation and mutual support were essential for facing challenges and ensuring the group's well-being. Reciprocal behavior, such as sharing food, providing assistance, or offering protection, helped foster strong social bonds and increased the chances of survival for both individuals and the community as a whole.

Psychologically, reciprocity is driven by a complex interplay of emotions, social norms, and cognitive processes. When we receive a favor or gift, we experience a sense of gratitude and indebtedness. These feelings create a psychological discomfort that can be alleviated by reciprocating the gesture. By returning the favor, we not only express our appreciation but also maintain a sense of fairness and balance in our social interactions.

The norm of reciprocity is universal and can be observed across diverse cultures and social contexts. From the exchange of gifts in personal relationships to the negotiation of business deals, reciprocity plays a significant role in shaping our interactions and decision-making processes. Anthropological studies have documented the presence of reciprocal behavior in various societies, ranging from hunter-gatherer communities to modern industrialized nations.

In the context of business and professional relationships, understanding and leveraging the principle of reciprocity can be a powerful tool for building trust, fostering collaboration, and achieving mutual success. By providing value and assistance to others, we create a social obligation that can lead to reciprocal actions in our favor. This can manifest in various forms, such as referrals, partnerships, or even increased loyalty from clients and customers.

Throughout this chapter, we will explore the psychology of reciprocity in greater depth and examine how you can harness its power to create meaningful connections and accelerate your business growth through your book. By understanding the underlying mechanisms and strategies involved, you will be better equipped to create a book that not only provides value to your readers but also sets the stage for mutually beneficial relationships and opportunities.

The Power of Giving in Business Relationships

In the world of business, building strong, lasting relationships is essential for success. One of the most effective ways to foster these relationships is through the power of giving. When you genuinely give to others, whether it's your time, expertise, or resources, you create a sense of obligation and goodwill that can have far-reaching effects on your professional life.

When you give to others in a business context, you demonstrate that you value their needs and are willing to invest in their success. This selfless act of generosity can create a powerful psychological response in the recipient. They feel appreciated, supported, and indebted to you in a positive way. This sense of obligation is not a burden but rather a desire to reciprocate your kindness and support.

The impact of giving extends beyond the immediate recipient. When others witness your generosity or hear about it through word-of-mouth, they form a positive impression of you and your business. They perceive you as someone who is not solely focused on personal gain but rather as an individual who prioritizes the well-being and success of others. This reputation can open doors to new opportunities, partnerships, and clients who are drawn to your giving mindset.

Embracing a giving mindset in business has numerous long-term benefits. By consistently providing value to others, you establish yourself as a trusted and reliable resource in your industry. People are more likely to seek out your expertise, refer others to you, and engage in mutually beneficial collaborations. Furthermore, a giving approach fosters a positive and supportive business environment, which can lead to increased productivity, creativity, and overall job satisfaction for you and your team.

To incorporate generosity into your professional interactions, consider the following strategies:

1. Share your knowledge and expertise freely. Offer valuable insights, advice, or resources to your clients, colleagues, and industry peers without expecting anything in return.
2. Be a connector. Introduce people in your network who could benefit from knowing each other. By facilitating meaningful connections, you create value for multiple parties and strengthen your own relationships in the process.
3. Offer complimentary services or resources. Consider providing a free consultation, a helpful template, or a valuable re-

source to demonstrate your commitment to your clients' success.

4. Volunteer your time and skills. Participate in industry events, mentor aspiring professionals, or contribute to charitable causes aligned with your values. By giving back to your community, you not only make a positive impact but also expand your network and enhance your reputation.

5. Express gratitude and appreciation. Acknowledge the contributions and successes of others in your professional circle. Celebrate their achievements, provide genuine praise, and offer support during challenging times.

By incorporating these strategies into your business practices, you create a culture of generosity that permeates your interactions and relationships. Over time, this giving mindset becomes an integral part of your brand and sets you apart from competitors who prioritize self-interest over the well-being of others.

Your Book as the Ultimate Gift

In the realm of business relationships, few things can make a more lasting and profound impact than giving your book as a gift. Your book is not just a tangible object; it is a manifestation of your expertise, insights, and dedication to your craft. By positioning your book as a valuable and meaningful gift, you create a powerful tool for building rapport, establishing credibility, and fostering long-term relationships with your clients and prospects.

When you share your book with others, you are essentially gifting them a piece of yourself. Your book encapsulates your unique perspective, hard-earned knowledge, and practical strategies that have been distilled through years of experience. By offering this wealth of information and insights, you demonstrate your generosity and willingness to go above and beyond to support your audience's growth and success.

The impact of sharing your expertise through your book cannot be overstated. When your clients or prospects read your book, they gain a deeper understanding of your thought process, methodology, and the value you bring to the table. They discover actionable insights and strategies that they can immediately apply to their own challenges and goals. By providing this level of value upfront, you establish yourself as a trusted authority and demonstrate your commitment to their success.

Giving your book as a gift also sets you apart from competitors who may rely solely on traditional sales pitches or generic marketing materials. Your book is a unique and personalized offering that showcases your expertise in a tangible and engaging format. It provides your audience with a comprehensive resource they can refer to repeatedly, reinforcing your message and strengthening your relationship with them over time.

The act of giving your book demonstrates your genuine interest in your audience's growth and success. It shows that you are not merely focused on closing a sale or securing a client but rather on providing long-term value and support. This commitment to their well-being can foster a deep sense of trust, loyalty, and appreciation, leading to stronger and more fruitful business relationships.

To effectively position your book as the ultimate gift, consider the following strategies:

1. Personalize your book with a thoughtful inscription. Take the time to write a personalized message that speaks directly to the recipient's unique needs, challenges, or aspirations. This small gesture can make a significant impact and show that you value them as an individual.
2. Pair your book with a complementary resource or offer. Consider bundling your book with an additional resource, such as a workbook, template, or exclusive access to a webinar or coaching session. This added value reinforces the comprehensive nature of your expertise and support.

3. Use your book as a follow-up or thank-you gift. After a meaningful interaction or milestone with a client or prospect, surprise them with a copy of your book as a token of appreciation. This unexpected gesture can deepen your connection and leave a lasting positive impression.

4. Create a customized book experience. For high-value clients or prospects, consider creating a bespoke version of your book that includes personalized insights, case studies, or recommendations tailored to their specific industry or challenges. This level of customization showcases your commitment to their unique success.

By leveraging your book as the ultimate gift, you create a powerful catalyst for building strong, enduring relationships with your clients and prospects. Your generosity and expertise will be remembered and appreciated long after the initial gift is given, setting the stage for ongoing collaboration, referrals, and business growth.

The Psychological Impact of a Signed Copy

In the world of business and authorship, a signed copy of your book holds a special power. It transforms your book from a valuable resource into a cherished and personal keepsake. The simple act of signing your book adds a layer of authenticity, exclusivity, and emotional connection that can significantly enhance the impact of your gift and strengthen the bond between you and your reader.

When you present a signed copy of your book to a client or prospect, you are offering them a piece of yourself. Your signature is a tangible representation of your personal brand, your commitment to your work, and your connection to the reader. It signifies that you have taken the time and effort to create a unique and personalized experience for them, elevating the perceived value of your book and your expertise.

A signed book carries a sense of exclusivity and rarity. In a world where digital content is abundant and easily accessible, a signed physical copy stands out as a limited-edition item. Your reader understands that they are receiving something special and exclusive, which heightens their appreciation and attachment to your book and, by extension, to you as the author and expert.

Moreover, a signed copy strengthens the emotional connection between you and your reader. By personalizing the book with a heartfelt inscription or message, you create a moment of intimacy and shared experience. Your reader feels seen, valued, and connected to you on a deeper level. They understand that you have taken the time to consider their unique needs and aspirations, fostering a sense of trust and loyalty that can extend far beyond the pages of your book.

Just as fans eagerly seek out autographs from their favorite celebrities, your readers will perceive you as a celebrity expert in your field when you offer them a signed copy of your book. This elevated status reinforces your authority, credibility, and influence in their eyes. By providing a personalized and autographed book, you are not only sharing your expertise but also creating a memorable and exclusive experience that sets you apart from others in your industry.

To maximize the impact of a signed copy, consider the following strategies:

1. Create a memorable and meaningful inscription. Take a moment to reflect on your reader's unique qualities, challenges, or goals. Craft a personalized message that speaks directly to their situation and offers encouragement, support, or inspiration. This level of customization shows that you genuinely care about their success and well-being.
2. Use high-quality materials and packaging. Invest in a high-quality pen and ink that will stand the test of time. Consider using a custom bookplate or stamp to add a professional and polished touch to your signature. Present your signed book in an attractive gift box or wrapped in elegant paper to enhance the overall presentation and create a memorable unboxing experience.

3. Include a personal note or letter. In addition to signing your book, consider including a handwritten note or letter that expresses your gratitude, shares a relevant anecdote, or offers further guidance or support. This extra touch reinforces the personal nature of your gift and demonstrates your willingness to go above and beyond for your reader.

4. Offer a virtual signing experience. In situations where a physical signing may not be possible, consider offering a virtual signing experience. This can involve creating a personalized video message or hosting a live virtual signing event where you can interact with your readers in real-time. By leveraging technology, you can still create a sense of personal connection and exclusivity, even from a distance.

The psychological impact of a signed copy cannot be underestimated. It elevates your status as an expert and thought leader, making you the celebrity in your reader's eyes. By harnessing the power of a signed copy, you create a lasting impression that extends beyond the initial gift. Your reader will feel valued, supported, and motivated to take action based on your insights and guidance. They will be more likely to share their positive experience with others, become loyal advocates for your brand, and seek out further opportunities to engage with you and your work.

Balancing Generosity and Business Objectives

While giving your book as a gift can be a powerful tool for building relationships and establishing your authority, it's essential to approach this strategy with authenticity and balance. Genuine generosity should be at the core of your book gifting efforts, rather than a purely transactional mindset. When you focus on providing value and making a positive impact on your readers, the business benefits will naturally follow.

To ensure that your book gifting aligns with your business objectives while maintaining authentic generosity, consider the following strategies:

1. Lead with value. Always prioritize providing value to your readers above promoting your own interests. When selecting recipients for your book gift, consider how your expertise and insights can genuinely help them overcome challenges, achieve their goals, or grow in their personal or professional lives. By leading with a sincere desire to make a difference, your generosity will shine through.

2. Customize your approach. Tailor your book gifting strategy to align with your specific business goals and target audience. Consider the most appropriate times and contexts to share your book, such as during client onboarding, as a thank-you for referrals, or as part of a larger marketing campaign. By customizing your approach, you can ensure that your book gifting feels relevant and valuable to your recipients.

3. Focus on long-term relationships. View book gifting as an investment in building long-term relationships rather than a one-time transaction. Instead of expecting immediate returns, focus on cultivating genuine connections and providing ongoing value to your readers. This long-term perspective will help you avoid coming across as self-serving or manipulative and instead foster trust and loyalty.

4. Measure success holistically. While it's important to track metrics such as sales, client acquisition, and revenue growth, don't overlook the intangible benefits of book gifting. Consider success stories that demonstrate the impact of your book on your readers' lives, such as positive feedback, testimonials, or meaningful connections formed. These qualitative measures can be just as valuable as quantitative ones in assessing the effectiveness of your book gifting strategy.

5. Provide value beyond the book. Extend your generosity beyond the initial book gift by offering additional resources, support, or engagement opportunities. This could include invitations to exclusive events, access to complementary materials, or personalized follow-up conversations. By continuing to provide value and support, you reinforce your commit-

ment to your readers' success and strengthen the relationships formed through your book.

To illustrate the power of balancing generosity and business objectives, consider the following success story:

Sarah, a leadership coach and consultant, wrote a book on effective communication strategies for executives. As part of her book gifting strategy, she identified key clients and prospects who she believed would benefit most from her insights. She personalized each book with a heartfelt inscription and included a handwritten note expressing her appreciation for their partnership and her commitment to their success.

In the months following her book gifting campaign, Sarah received numerous messages from recipients expressing gratitude for the valuable insights and practical strategies they gained from her book. Several clients reached out to discuss how they had implemented her advice and seen positive results in their organizations. Some even referred new clients to Sarah, citing her book as a testament to her expertise and generosity.

By leading with authentic generosity and focusing on providing value, Sarah was able to strengthen her client relationships, attract new business, and establish herself as a trusted authority in her field. Her success demonstrates the power of balancing generosity and business objectives in a book gifting strategy.

When executed with authenticity and care, giving your book as a gift can be a transformative tool for building relationships, establishing your authority, and achieving your business goals. By prioritizing genuine generosity and focusing on the long-term impact, you can create a powerful cycle of reciprocity that benefits both you and your readers.

Real-World Examples of Reciprocity in Action

To further illustrate the power of reciprocity in business relationships, let's explore a few real-world examples of businesses and authors who have successfully leveraged this principle. By analyzing the specific tactics and approaches used in each case study, we can extract valuable lessons and insights that you can apply to your own book gifting strategy.

Case Study 1: The Consultant's Game-Changing Book Jennifer, a management consultant, wrote a book on effective leadership strategies for small businesses. As part of her book gifting campaign, she identified a list of 50 key prospects who she believed could benefit from her expertise. She personalized each book with a handwritten note and included an invitation to a complimentary one-hour consultation session.

The response was overwhelming. Over 60% of the recipients took Jennifer up on her offer for a consultation, and many expressed gratitude for the valuable insights they gained from her book. Several of these consultations led to long-term consulting engagements, and Jennifer saw a significant increase in her business revenue as a result.

Key takeaway: Combining your book gift with a complementary offering, such as a consultation or strategy session, can create a powerful reciprocity effect and open doors to new business opportunities.

Case Study 2: The Coach's Referral Boom Mark, a business coach, wrote a book on effective networking strategies for entrepreneurs. He decided to give copies of his book to his existing clients as a token of appreciation for their business and loyalty. Inside each book, he included a personalized thank-you note, and a request for referrals if they found the book valuable.

Within a month, Mark received a flood of referrals from his clients. Many shared how the book had helped them improve their networking skills and expressed their gratitude by recommending Mark's coaching services to their colleagues and friends. As a result, Mark's client base grew by 25% in the following quarter.

Key takeaway: Gifting your book to existing clients can strengthen relationships, generate goodwill, and lead to a surge in referrals and new business opportunities.

Case Study 3: The Author's Speaking Engagement Success Sarah, a motivational speaker and author, wrote a book on overcoming adversity and achieving personal growth. She decided to leverage her book as a tool to secure more speaking engagements. Prior to each event, she would send a personalized copy of her book to the event organizer, along with a heartfelt note expressing her excitement for the upcoming presentation.

The response was incredible. Event organizers were impressed by Sarah's generosity and often shared their appreciation for the book with their audience during the introduction. Many attendees approached Sarah after her presentations to purchase additional copies of her book and inquire about her coaching services. As a result, Sarah's speaking career flourished, and she became a sought-after expert in her field.

Key takeaway: Using your book as a thoughtful gift prior to speaking engagements or other professional events can create a positive impression, enhance your credibility, and lead to additional opportunities for growth and exposure.

These real-world examples demonstrate the power of reciprocity in action. By analyzing the specific tactics and approaches used in each case study, we can identify common themes and best practices:

1. Personalization: Each example showcased the importance of personalizing the book gift with a heartfelt note or inscription, making the recipient feel valued and appreciated.
2. Complementary offerings: Combining the book gift with a complementary offering, such as a consultation or additional resources, can amplify the reciprocity effect and encourage further engagement.

3. Targeted outreach: Identifying key prospects, clients, or influencers who are most likely to benefit from and appreciate your book can lead to higher response rates and more meaningful connections.
4. Authentic generosity: In each case, the authors, and businesses approached their book gifting with a spirit of genuine generosity, focusing on providing value and making a positive impact rather than solely seeking personal gain.

By incorporating these lessons and best practices into your own book gifting strategy, you can harness the power of reciprocity to build stronger relationships, generate goodwill, and unlock new opportunities for your business.

Chapter 5

Using Your Book in Your Sales Process

A well-defined sales process is the backbone of any successful business. It provides a clear roadmap for guiding potential clients from initial contact to closing the deal. By mapping out your current sales process, you can identify opportunities to integrate your book and enhance your overall sales strategy.

A well-structured sales process helps you:

- Ensure consistency in your sales approach
- Identify bottlenecks and areas for improvement
- Forecast sales more accurately
- Train and onboard new sales team members effectively
- Measure and optimize your sales performance

Investing time in understanding and refining your sales process is crucial for leveraging your book as a powerful sales tool.

Identifying the Key Stages and Touchpoints in Your Current Sales Process

To effectively integrate your book into your sales process, you first need to identify the key stages and touchpoints in your current approach. While sales processes may vary depending on your industry and business model, most typically include the following stages:

1. Prospecting: Identifying and reaching out to potential clients who may benefit from your products or services.
2. Qualification: Assessing whether a prospect is a good fit for your offerings based on their needs, budget, and decision-making authority.
3. Presentation: Demonstrating the value of your products or services through presentations, proposals, or demos.
4. Objection Handling: Addressing any concerns or hesitations the prospect may have about moving forward with your solution.
5. Closing: Securing the prospect's commitment to purchase and finalizing the deal.
6. Follow-up: Nurturing the relationship with the new client and ensuring their satisfaction with your products or services.

By mapping out these stages and the specific touchpoints within each stage, you can pinpoint the most effective moments to introduce and leverage your book in the sales process.

Assessing the Strengths and Weaknesses of Your Existing Approach

With a clear understanding of your current sales process, you can assess its strengths and weaknesses. This introspection will help you identify areas where your book can make the most significant impact.

Consider the following questions:

- Which stages of your sales process are most effective in converting prospects to clients?
- Are there any stages where prospects consistently lose interest or disengage?
- Do you have a standardized approach for each stage, or does it vary depending on the salesperson?
- Are there any specific objections or concerns that arise frequently during the sales process?
- How do you currently differentiate yourself from competitors during the sales process?

By answering these questions honestly, you can uncover opportunities to use your book strategically to enhance your sales process. For example, if prospects often lose interest during the presentation stage, you could use your book as a compelling leave-behind to keep them engaged. If you struggle to differentiate yourself from competitors, highlighting your book can help establish your unique authority and expertise. By leveraging your book strategically throughout the sales journey, you can transform your sales process and achieve unprecedented business growth.

Identifying Key Moments to Introduce Your Book

To maximize the impact of your book on your sales process, it's essential to identify the key moments when introducing your book can make the most significant difference. These optimal points will vary depending on your specific sales process and the nature of your business, but there are several critical junctures where your book can be particularly effective.

One of the most opportune moments to introduce your book is during the prospecting stage. By offering your book as a valuable resource to potential clients, you can establish your credibility and thought leadership from the outset. This can be especially powerful if your book addresses the specific pain points or challenges that your target audience faces, demonstrating that you understand their needs and have the expertise to help them succeed.

Another crucial point to leverage your book is during the presentation stage. By incorporating insights and case studies from your book into your sales presentations, you can differentiate yourself from competitors and provide tangible evidence of your ability to deliver results. This can help build trust and confidence in your offerings, making prospects more likely to choose your solutions over others.

Considering the Customer Journey and Decision-Making Process

To determine the most effective moments to introduce your book, it's important to consider the customer journey and decision-making process. By understanding the steps your prospects take as they move from awareness to consideration to decision, you can align your book's content and positioning with their needs and mindset at each stage.

For example, during the awareness stage, prospects may be just beginning to recognize their problems or challenges. At this point, your book can serve as a valuable resource for educating them about the issues they face and the potential solutions available. By providing helpful, informative content that speaks to their needs, you can establish your expertise and build trust early in the customer journey.

As prospects move into the consideration stage, they begin to evaluate their options more seriously. This is where your book can be used to showcase your unique approach and the benefits of working with you. By highlighting case studies and success stories from your book, you can demonstrate the tangible results you've achieved for other clients and help prospects envision the impact you could have on their own business.

Finally, when prospects reach the decision stage, your book can be a powerful tool for overcoming any lingering objections and reinforcing the value of your offerings. By addressing common concerns and providing a clear roadmap for success, your book can give prospects the confidence they need to move forward with your solutions.

Aligning Your Book's Content with Specific Sales Stages and Objectives

To effectively leverage your book at each stage of the sales process, it's crucial to align your book's content with the specific objectives and challenges prospects face at each juncture. This requires a deep understanding of your target audience and their unique needs, as well as a clear strategy for how your book can address those needs.

One effective approach is to map out the key themes and insights from your book and match them to the corresponding stages of the sales process. For example, if your book includes a chapter on common mistakes businesses make in your industry, you could use that content to help prospects identify areas for improvement during the awareness stage. Similarly, if your book features case studies of successful client engagements, you could highlight those examples during the consideration stage to showcase your expertise and results.

By carefully curating the content and messaging from your book to align with each stage of the sales process, you can create a seamless, integrated sales experience that leverages the full power of your thought leadership. This strategic alignment not only enhances the effectiveness of your sales efforts but also reinforces the value and relevance of your book throughout the customer journey.

Ultimately, identifying the key moments to introduce your book in your sales process requires a deep understanding of your target audience, your unique offerings, and the specific challenges and objectives at each stage of the customer journey. By strategically aligning your book's content with these critical junctures, you can unlock its full potential as a sales tool and drive meaningful results for your business.

Using Your Book as a Lead Magnet and Conversation Starter

One of the most powerful ways to leverage your book in the sales process is by using it as a lead magnet to attract and engage potential clients. By offering your book as a valuable resource, you can demonstrate your expertise, build trust, and establish a meaningful connection with prospects from the very beginning of your relationship.

To effectively use your book as a lead magnet, consider the following strategies:

1. Offer a free chapter or excerpt: Provide a compelling snippet of your book that addresses a specific challenge or pain point your target audience faces. This can help generate interest and encourage prospects to engage further with your content.
2. Create a landing page: Develop a dedicated landing page that highlights the key benefits and insights readers will gain from your book. Use persuasive copy and clear calls-to-action to encourage visitors to provide their contact information in exchange for a free copy or chapter of your book.
3. Leverage social media: Share quotes, excerpts, and key takeaways from your book on your social media channels. Encourage followers to download a free chapter or request a copy of your book to learn more.
4. Offer a book club or discussion guide: Create a complementary resource that helps readers engage more deeply with your book's content. This can include discussion questions, worksheets, or additional insights that encourage prospects to explore your ideas further.

By offering your book as a valuable resource, you not only attract potential clients but also position yourself as a generous, knowledgeable expert who is committed to helping others succeed.

Crafting Compelling Offers and Calls-to-Action Around Your Book

To maximize the effectiveness of your book as a lead magnet, it's essential to craft compelling offers and calls-to-action that encourage prospects to take the next step in engaging with your business. This requires a clear understanding of your target audience's needs and desires, as well as a persuasive value proposition that highlights the benefits of your book.

When crafting your offers and calls-to-action, consider the following tips:

1. Focus on benefits, not just features: Instead of simply describing what your book contains, emphasize the tangible benefits and outcomes readers will experience by engaging with your content. Will they gain a competitive edge, solve a pressing problem, or achieve a specific goal?
2. Create a sense of urgency: Use language that encourages prospects to take action now, rather than putting it off for later. This can include time-limited offers, exclusive bonuses, or a limited supply of free copies.
3. Make it easy to take action: Ensure that your calls-to-action are clear, concise, and easy to follow. Use prominent buttons, simple forms, and straightforward instructions to minimize friction and encourage prospects to take the desired action.
4. Test and optimize: Continuously monitor the performance of your offers and calls-to-action, and be willing to experiment with different approaches. Use A/B testing to identify the most effective messaging, design, and placement for your specific audience.

By crafting compelling offers and calls-to-action around your book, you can convert more prospects into leads and set the stage for meaningful conversations and relationships.

Using Your Book to Initiate Meaningful Conversations and Build Rapport

Beyond serving as a lead magnet, your book can also be a powerful tool for initiating meaningful conversations and building rapport with potential clients. By sharing your insights and experiences through your book, you create a natural opening for deeper discussions and relationships.

Consider the following approaches for using your book to spark meaningful conversations:

1. Ask for feedback and insights: When sharing your book with prospects, invite them to provide their thoughts, questions, and experiences related to the topics you cover. This can lead to rich discussions that help you better understand their needs and perspectives.
2. Share personal anecdotes: Use stories and examples from your book as a starting point for sharing your own experiences and insights. This can help humanize your expertise and create a more personal, relatable connection with prospects.
3. Offer a complimentary consultation: Use your book as a springboard for offering a free consultation or strategy session. This provides an opportunity to dive deeper into the prospect's specific challenges and explore how your services can help them achieve their goals.
4. Host a book club or webinar: Bring prospects together for a group discussion or online event centered around your book. This can foster a sense of community and shared learning, while also positioning you as a facilitator and expert in your field.

By using your book to initiate meaningful conversations and build rapport, you lay the foundation for strong, trusting relationships with potential clients. This authentic, value-driven approach can differentiate you from competitors and set the stage for long-term partnerships and success.

Leveraging Your Book in Sales Meetings and Presentations

Your book is a powerful tool for demonstrating your expertise and providing value to potential clients during sales meetings and presentations. By strategically incorporating your book's key concepts and frameworks into these discussions, you can differentiate yourself from competitors and showcase the unique insights and solutions you bring to the table.

To effectively integrate your book's content into sales conversations, consider the following strategies:

1. Identify relevant concepts and frameworks: Prior to each sales meeting, review your book's content and identify the specific concepts, models, or frameworks that are most relevant to the prospect's needs and challenges. This targeted approach ensures that your book's insights are directly applicable and valuable to the discussion at hand.

2. Use your book as a reference point: When introducing key concepts or ideas, refer back to specific chapters or sections of your book. This not only reinforces your credibility as an author but also provides a tangible resource that prospects can explore further after the meeting.

3. Share real-world examples and case studies: Use stories and examples from your book to illustrate how your ideas have been successfully applied in practice. This helps prospects visualize the potential impact of your solutions and builds trust in your ability to deliver results.

4. Encourage questions and discussion: Rather than simply presenting your book's content, use it as a starting point for engaging prospects in meaningful dialogue. Encourage them to ask questions, share their own experiences, and explore how your book's concepts relate to their specific situation.

By seamlessly incorporating your book's concepts and frameworks into sales discussions, you can elevate the quality and impact of your conversations, demonstrating the value and relevance of your expertise.

Using Your Book as a Visual Aid and Reference Tool During Meetings

In addition to verbally referencing your book's content, using it as a visual aid and reference tool during sales meetings can enhance the impact and memorability of your presentations. By physically sharing your book and highlighting key passages or illustrations, you create a more engaging and interactive experience for prospects.

Consider the following ways to use your book as a visual aid:

1. Bring physical copies to meetings: Provide each attendee with a copy of your book, or have several on hand to reference during the discussion. This not only makes your book's content more tangible but also serves as a valuable leave-behind for prospects to review and share with others.
2. Bookmark key pages or passages: Prior to the meeting, identify the specific pages or sections of your book that are most relevant to the prospect's needs. Use bookmarks, sticky notes, or other visual cues to quickly reference these key points during the discussion.
3. Project digital excerpts or illustrations: If meeting virtually or in a room with presentation capabilities, consider projecting key excerpts, diagrams, or illustrations from your book onto a screen. This allows you to visually highlight important concepts and make your book's content more engaging and accessible.
4. Create companion slides or handouts: Develop complementary visual aids, such as slides or handouts, that summarize key ideas from your book and align with your sales presentation. These materials can help reinforce your book's content and provide prospects with additional resources to reference after the meeting.

By using your book as a visual aid and reference tool, you can create a more immersive and memorable sales experience that strengthens the impact of your expertise and ideas.

Demonstrating Your Expertise and Credibility Through Your Book's Content

Ultimately, your book is a powerful tool for demonstrating your expertise and credibility in your field. By sharing the insights, experiences, and success stories captured in your book, you can build trust with prospects and differentiate yourself as a true authority and thought leader.

To maximize the impact of your book in demonstrating your expertise, consider the following approaches:

1. Highlight your unique perspective and methodology: Use your book to showcase the distinctive ideas, frameworks, and approaches that set you apart from others in your industry. By emphasizing your unique perspective, you position yourself as an innovator and leader in your field.
2. Share client success stories and testimonials: Include powerful case studies and testimonials from clients who have successfully implemented your book's strategies and achieved significant results. These real-world examples provide compelling social proof of your expertise and the effectiveness of your approach.
3. Demonstrate your thought leadership: Highlight sections of your book that address emerging trends, challenges, or opportunities in your industry. By sharing your forward-thinking insights and predictions, you demonstrate your deep understanding of the market, and your ability to help clients stay ahead of the curve.
4. Provide value-added resources: Offer prospects additional resources, such as worksheets, templates, or assessments, that complement your book's content and help them apply your ideas in practice. These value-added materials further showcase your expertise and commitment to client success.

By leveraging your book's content to demonstrate your expertise and credibility, you can build deeper trust and confidence with prospects, positioning yourself as the go-to partner for achieving their goals and overcoming their challenges.

Following Up After Your Book Has Been Received

Giving your book to a potential client is a significant milestone in the sales process, but it's just the beginning of the relationship-building journey. To maximize the impact of your book and convert prospects into clients, it's essential to follow up in a timely and personalized manner after they have received your book.

Prompt follow-up demonstrates your commitment to the relationship and your genuine interest in the prospect's success. It also allows you to:

1. Ensure the book was received: Following up confirms that your book reached the prospect and provides an opportunity to address any issues or questions they may have.
2. Gauge initial reactions and feedback: Checking in after the prospect has had time to review your book allows you to gather valuable insights into their thoughts and reactions. This feedback can help you tailor your approach and address any concerns or objections early on.
3. Reinforce key messages and value: By highlighting specific aspects of your book that align with the prospect's needs, you can reinforce the value and relevance of your expertise and solutions.
4. Set the stage for next steps: Following up opens the door for discussing how your book's ideas can be applied to the prospect's specific situation and what steps they can take to move forward.

To ensure your follow-up is effective and well-received, consider the following best practices:

- Personalize your outreach: Avoid generic follow-up messages and instead tailor your communication to the specific prospect and their unique needs and interests.
- Be timely and respectful: Follow up within a reasonable timeframe after the prospect has received your book, while being mindful of their schedule and communication preferences.
- Provide value: Focus on how your book's insights can help the prospect achieve their goals, rather than simply pushing for a sale.

By prioritizing timely and personalized follow-up, you can deepen the connection with prospects and set the stage for a productive, mutually beneficial relationship.

Strategies for Checking In and Gathering Feedback on Your Book's Impact

Following up after your book has been received is an invaluable opportunity to gather feedback and insights into how your ideas have resonated with the prospect. This feedback not only helps you gauge the impact of your book but also provides valuable information for tailoring your approach and offering relevant solutions.

Consider the following strategies for checking in and gathering feedback:

1. Ask open-ended questions: Encourage prospects to share their thoughts and reactions by asking open-ended questions such as, "What insights from the book resonated with you most?" or "How do you see the book's ideas applying to your current challenges?"
2. Offer a feedback survey: Provide a simple feedback form or survey that prospects can complete to share their opinions and suggestions. This can include rating scales, multiple-choice questions, and open comment fields for more detailed responses.

3. Schedule a follow-up discussion: Invite the prospect to a brief phone or video call to discuss their reactions to your book in more depth. This allows for a more interactive and personalized conversation, while also demonstrating your commitment to their success.

4. Share success stories: If you have testimonials or case studies from other clients who have implemented your book's ideas, share these with the prospect. This social proof can help reinforce the value of your approach and encourage the prospect to provide their own feedback.

5. Offer a book club or discussion guide: Provide a structured way for prospects to engage with your book's content and share their insights. This can include discussion questions, prompts for reflection, or exercises for applying your ideas in practice.

By proactively seeking feedback and creating opportunities for prospects to share their thoughts, you demonstrate your genuine interest in their perspective and lay the foundation for a collaborative, customer-centric relationship.

Leveraging Your Book as a Reason to Continue the Conversation and Nurture the Relationship

Beyond gathering feedback, following up after your book has been received is a natural opportunity to continue the conversation and nurture the relationship with the prospect. By using your book as a touchstone for ongoing dialogue, you can deepen the connection and move the prospect closer to becoming a client.

Consider the following ways to leverage your book for continued conversation and relationship-building:

1. Offer a complementary consultation: Use the prospect's feedback and questions about your book as a springboard for offering a complementary consultation or strategy session. This allows you to dive deeper into their specific needs

and demonstrate how your expertise can help them achieve their goals.

2. Invite them to a webinar or event: If you have upcoming webinars, workshops, or other events related to your book's topics, invite the prospect to attend as your guest. This provides additional value and opportunities for engagement, while also positioning you as a generous and committed partner.

3. Share relevant articles or resources: As you come across articles, case studies, or other resources that relate to your book's ideas, and the prospect's interests, share these with a personalized note. This demonstrates your ongoing thought leadership and commitment to providing value.

4. Offer a sneak peek of upcoming content: If you have plans for a follow-up book, course, or other content related to your book's themes, share a preview or excerpt with the prospect. This exclusive access can deepen their engagement and excitement about your ongoing work.

5. Celebrate their progress and successes: As the prospect begins to implement your book's ideas and achieves positive results, celebrate their progress and successes. This could include featuring them in a case study, sharing their story on social media, or simply sending a personalized note of congratulations.

By leveraging your book as a reason to continue the conversation and nurture the relationship, you can build a strong foundation of trust, value, and collaboration with the prospect. This ongoing dialogue positions you as a trusted partner and advisor, rather than just another vendor or salesperson.

Effective follow-up is essential for maximizing the impact of your book in the sales process. By prioritizing timely and personalized outreach, gathering valuable feedback, and using your book as a springboard for ongoing conversation and relationship-building, you can convert more prospects into loyal clients and advocates for your business.

Transitioning from Book Discussion to Sales Conversation

Once you've engaged a prospect in a meaningful discussion about your book, the next step is to skillfully transition the conversation towards your product or service offerings. This pivot point is critical, as it allows you to build upon the trust and credibility established through your book and demonstrate how your expertise can directly address the prospect's needs.

To smoothly pivot from book-related topics to sales discussions, consider the following techniques:

1. Ask probing questions: Use the book discussion as an opportunity to ask thoughtful, open-ended questions that uncover the prospect's specific challenges, goals, and pain points. By actively listening and showing genuine curiosity, you can naturally steer the conversation towards how your offerings can provide solutions.

2. Highlight relevant case studies: Share brief examples or case studies from your book that showcase how other clients have successfully overcome similar challenges using your approach. This helps the prospect visualize the potential impact of your offerings on their own situation.

3. Offer a specific recommendation: Based on the prospect's feedback, and the insights gathered during the book discussion, offer a tailored recommendation for how your product or service can help them achieve their objectives. This personalized approach demonstrates your attentiveness and commitment to their success.

4. Invite them to a discovery session: Suggest a more focused, one-on-one discovery session to dive deeper into the prospect's unique needs and explore how your offerings can provide value. This allows for a natural progression from the book discussion to a more targeted sales conversation.

5. Provide a special offer: To encourage the prospect to take the next step, consider offering a special discount, bonus, or

trial related to your product or service. Position this as an exclusive opportunity for readers of your book, reinforcing the value of the relationship.

By employing these techniques, you can gracefully transition from the book discussion to a sales conversation without coming across as pushy or insincere. The key is to focus on the prospect's needs and how your expertise, as demonstrated in your book, can help them succeed.

Identifying Natural Opportunities to Segue into Your Product or Service Offerings

In addition to the above techniques, it's important to be attuned to natural opportunities that arise during the book discussion to segue into your product or service offerings. These organic openings allow you to introduce your solutions in a relevant and timely manner, without disrupting the flow of the conversation.

Some natural opportunities to watch for include:

1. The prospect expresses a specific challenge or pain point: When the prospect shares a struggle or obstacle they're facing, use this as a chance to highlight how your offerings can help address that particular issue. Offer a brief example or anecdote from your book that relates to their situation.
2. The prospect asks for your advice or recommendations: If the prospect directly seeks your guidance on a topic related to your expertise, use this as an opening to discuss your product or service as a potential solution. Share how your offerings have helped other clients in similar situations, and the specific benefits they can expect.
3. The prospect expresses interest in learning more: When the prospect shows curiosity or enthusiasm about a particular aspect of your book, use this as a springboard to delve into your related offerings. Offer to send additional information or resources that showcase how your product or service brings these ideas to life.

4. The prospect mentions a specific goal or aspiration: If the prospect shares a desired outcome or future vision, highlight how your offerings can help them achieve that goal more efficiently or effectively. Use examples from your book to illustrate the potential impact and value of your approach.

By staying alert to these natural opportunities and seamlessly integrating your product or service into the conversation, you can create a more organic and persuasive sales pitch that feels authentic and customer-centric.

Handling Objections and Concerns That May Arise During the Transition

As you navigate the transition from book discussion to sales conversation, it's natural for prospects to raise objections or concerns. These may relate to pricing, timing, fit, or other factors that could impede their decision to move forward. Handling these objections with empathy, transparency, and a focus on value is key to maintaining trust and moving the sales process forward.

Consider the following strategies for addressing common objections and concerns:

1. Acknowledge and validate their perspective: Show that you understand and appreciate the prospect's concerns by actively listening and acknowledging their point of view. This helps build rapport and positions you as a collaborative partner, rather than an adversary.
2. Reframe the objection as an opportunity: Instead of viewing objections as roadblocks, reframe them as opportunities to provide further clarity and value. For example, if a prospect balks at pricing, use this as a chance to highlight the unique benefits and ROI of your offerings compared to alternatives.
3. Provide social proof and evidence: Use case studies, testimonials, and data from your book to address specific objections and demonstrate the real-world impact of your offerings. This helps build credibility and trust in your solutions.

4. Offer a trial or pilot: If the prospect is hesitant to commit to a full engagement, suggest a smaller-scale trial or pilot project to demonstrate value and mitigate risk. This allows them to experience your offerings firsthand and builds momentum for a larger partnership.
5. Emphasize the cost of inaction: Gently remind the prospect of the potential consequences of not addressing their challenges or seizing opportunities related to your offerings. Use examples from your book to illustrate the impact of inaction, and the benefits of proactive change.

By approaching objections and concerns with empathy, transparency, and a focus on value, you can build trust and credibility with prospects even in the face of resistance. The goal is not to pressure or manipulate, but rather to provide the information and assurance needed for the prospect to make an informed and confident decision.

Transitioning from book discussion to sales conversation is a critical moment in the customer journey. By leveraging the techniques outlined above and staying attuned to natural opportunities for introducing your offerings, you can create a seamless and persuasive sales pitch that builds upon the trust and credibility established through your book. Handling objections and concerns with grace, and a focus on value will further strengthen the relationship and increase the likelihood of a successful partnership.

Using Your Book to Overcome Objections and Build Trust

One of the most powerful ways to leverage your book in the sales process is by using its content and case studies to proactively address and overcome common objections. By anticipating the concerns and hesitations that prospects may have and providing compelling evidence and examples from your book, you can build trust and credibility while positioning your offerings as the ideal solution.

To effectively address sales objections through your book, consider the following strategies:

1. Identify the most common objections: Reflect on your past sales conversations, and the recurring themes or concerns that prospects tend to raise. These may relate to pricing, timing, fit, or other factors that could impede their decision to move forward.

2. Map out relevant content and examples: Review your book's content and identify specific sections, case studies, or examples that directly address these common objections. Look for stories or data that illustrate how your approach has helped clients overcome similar challenges or achieve desired outcomes.

3. Incorporate objection-handling into your book discussion: When discussing your book with prospects, proactively highlight the sections or examples that relate to their specific concerns. This demonstrates your awareness of their needs and your proactive approach to addressing potential obstacles.

4. Provide tangible evidence and social proof: Use the case studies and examples from your book to provide concrete evidence of your offerings' impact and value. Share specific metrics, testimonials, or success stories that demonstrate how your solutions have helped clients achieve their goals and overcome objections.

5. Offer a clear roadmap or solution: In addition to highlighting relevant examples, use your book's content to provide a clear roadmap or solution for addressing the prospect's specific concerns. Outline the steps or strategies that have proven effective in similar situations and how your offerings can support their implementation.

By leveraging your book's content and case studies to proactively address and overcome objections, you can demonstrate your expertise, build trust, and position your offerings as the clear choice for the prospect's needs.

Leveraging Your Book's Authority and Credibility to Build Trust with Potential Clients

In addition to addressing specific objections, your book serves as a powerful tool for building overall trust and credibility with potential clients. By positioning you as a published authority in your field, your book lends weight to your ideas, recommendations, and offerings.

To leverage your book's authority and credibility in the sales process, consider the following approaches:

1. Highlight your book's unique perspective and insights: Emphasize the original research, frameworks, or viewpoints that your book brings to the table. This positions you as a thought leader and innovator in your industry, rather than just another vendor or service provider.
2. Showcase your book's endorsements and accolades: If your book has received endorsements from respected industry leaders, positive reviews, or awards, highlight these achievements in your sales conversations. This third-party validation reinforces your credibility and the value of your ideas.
3. Share your book's impact and reach: Provide statistics or anecdotes about your book's readership, global reach, or impact on your industry. This demonstrates the broader influence and acceptance of your ideas, building trust in your expertise.
4. Offer your book as a resource and guide: Position your book as a valuable resource and guide that prospects can refer to throughout their journey with your offerings. This reinforces your commitment to their success and your role as a trusted advisor and partner.
5. Integrate your book into your overall brand and messaging: Ensure that your book's key themes, frameworks, and messaging are consistently integrated into your broader sales and marketing efforts. This creates a cohesive and compelling brand narrative that builds trust and credibility across all touchpoints.

By leveraging your book's authority and credibility in these ways, you can differentiate yourself from competitors, build deeper trust with prospects, and position your offerings as the premium solution backed by a recognized expert.

Strategies for Using Your Book to Reframe Objections and Position Your Solutions Effectively

Beyond addressing objections directly, your book provides a valuable opportunity to reframe potential concerns and position your solutions in a more compelling and persuasive light. By using your book's content to shift the prospect's perspective and highlight the unique value of your offerings, you can overcome resistance and build a stronger case for partnership.

Consider the following strategies for using your book to reframe objections and position your solutions:

1. Reframe objections as opportunities: Use your book's content to reframe common objections as opportunities for growth, innovation, or competitive advantage. For example, if a prospect is concerned about the cost of your offerings, highlight examples from your book of how similar investments have yielded significant ROI or strategic benefits.
2. Highlight the cost of inaction: Use your book's case studies or cautionary tales to illustrate the potential consequences of not addressing the challenges or opportunities related to your offerings. This shifts the focus from the short-term costs to the long-term risks and benefits of taking action.
3. Emphasize your unique value proposition: Leverage your book's content to clearly articulate how your offerings are differentiated from competitors and uniquely suited to address the prospect's needs. Use specific examples or frameworks from your book to illustrate your distinctive approach, and the superior results it can deliver.
4. Position your offerings as a strategic investment: Frame your solutions not as a one-time expense, but as a strategic investment in the prospect's long-term success. Use your

book's content to highlight the broader impact and value of your offerings, such as improved efficiency, increased market share, or enhanced customer satisfaction.

5. Provide a clear path to success: Use your book's roadmaps, checklists, or action plans to provide a clear and tangible path for the prospect to achieve their desired outcomes with your offerings. This clarity and structure can help overcome objections related to uncertainty or complexity.

By leveraging your book's content to reframe objections and position your solutions in a more strategic and value-focused light, you can shift the conversation from potential barriers to potential breakthroughs. This approach not only helps overcome immediate concerns but also lays the foundation for a more productive and successful long-term partnership.

Using your book to overcome objections and build trust is a critical skill in the sales process. By addressing common concerns head-on, leveraging your book's authority and credibility, and reframing objections as opportunities, you can create a more compelling and persuasive case for your offerings. This approach not only helps you close more deals in the short term but also establishes you as a trusted advisor and partner for the long haul.

Measuring the Impact of Your Book on Your Sales Process

To truly understand the impact of your book on your sales process, it's essential to establish clear metrics and key performance indicators (KPIs) to track and measure its influence. By setting up a framework for monitoring your book's performance in the context of your sales efforts, you can gain valuable insights into what's working, what's not, and where there may be opportunities for improvement.

Consider tracking the following key metrics and KPIs:

1. Lead generation: Monitor the number of new leads generated through your book, such as prospects who download a free chapter, sign up for a webinar, or request a consultation after reading your book. Compare this to your lead generation rates prior to publishing your book to assess its impact on top-of-funnel activity.

2. Conversion rates: Track the percentage of book-related leads that convert into sales qualified leads, opportunities, and ultimately, closed deals. Analyze how these conversion rates compare to your overall sales funnel and whether your book is driving higher-quality leads that are more likely to convert.

3. Sales cycle length: Measure the average time it takes to move a book-related lead through your sales cycle, from initial contact to closed deal. Compare this to your typical sales cycle length to determine if your book is helping to accelerate the buying process and shorten the time to revenue.

4. Deal size: Evaluate the average deal size or contract value for clients who engage with your book during the sales process. Look for any correlations between book engagement and larger deal sizes, which may indicate that your book is helping to build trust and credibility, leading to more significant investments.

5. Customer lifetime value: Track the long-term value and loyalty of clients who were influenced by your book during the sales process. Monitor metrics such as retention rates, upsell/cross-sell opportunities, and customer referrals to assess the ongoing impact of your book on customer relationships.

By establishing these key metrics and KPIs, you can create a data-driven approach to measuring your book's impact on your sales process and make informed decisions about how to optimize its use for maximum results.

Analyzing Conversion Rates, Deal Sizes, and Sales Cycle Length Pre- and Post-Book

With your key metrics and KPIs in place, the next step is to conduct a comparative analysis of your sales performance before and after incorporating your book into your sales process. This analysis will help you quantify the tangible impact of your book and identify areas where it's having the greatest influence.

To analyze your conversion rates, deal sizes, and sales cycle length pre- and post-book, consider the following approach:

1. Define your timeframes: Determine the specific timeframes you want to compare, such as the 6–12 months before and after launching your book. Ensure that you have sufficient data within each timeframe to draw meaningful conclusions.

2. Segment your data: Separate your sales data into two segments: deals that involved your book in the sales process and deals that did not. This segmentation allows you to isolate the impact of your book and compare it to your baseline performance.

3. Calculate your metrics: For each segment and timeframe, calculate your key metrics, such as conversion rates at each stage of your sales funnel, average deal sizes, and average sales cycle length. Use this data to create a side-by-side comparison of your performance pre- and post-book.

4. Analyze the variances: Look for significant variances in your metrics between the pre- and post-book timeframes, as well as between the book-related and non-book-related segments. Identify any positive or negative changes in your conversion rates, deal sizes, or sales cycle length that may be attributable to your book.

5. Identify trends and patterns: Dive deeper into your data to uncover any notable trends or patterns related to your book's impact. For example, you may find that certain types of prospects or industries are more responsive to your book,

or that your book is particularly effective at a specific stage of the sales cycle.

By conducting this comparative analysis, you can gain a clearer picture of how your book is influencing your sales performance and where it's delivering the greatest ROI. Use these insights to refine your book-related sales strategies and double down on what's working best.

Gathering Qualitative Feedback from Clients and Sales Team Members on Your Book's Impact

In addition to quantitative metrics and data analysis, gathering qualitative feedback from clients and sales team members can provide valuable insights into how your book is being perceived and utilized in the sales process. This feedback can help you understand the more nuanced and subjective aspects of your book's impact and identify opportunities for improvement.

To gather qualitative feedback on your book's impact, consider the following strategies:

1. Client surveys and interviews: Reach out to clients who engaged with your book during the sales process and ask for their feedback through surveys or interviews. Ask open-ended questions about how your book influenced their decision-making process, what specific aspects resonated with them, and how it compared to other resources or materials they encountered during their buying journey.
2. Sales team debriefs: Conduct regular debriefs with your sales team members to gather their frontline insights on how your book is being used in sales conversations and how prospects are responding to it. Encourage them to share specific anecdotes or examples of how your book has helped to overcome objections, build trust, or accelerate deals.
3. Case studies and testimonials: Identify clients who have had particularly positive experiences with your book and ask them to participate in a case study or provide a testimonial.

These in-depth stories can provide valuable context and color around how your book has made a tangible impact on their business and their relationship with your company.

4. Social media and online reviews: Monitor social media mentions and online reviews related to your book to gather unsolicited feedback and sentiment from readers. Look for common themes or recurring praise or criticism that can help you understand how your book is being received and where there may be room for improvement.

5. Industry forums and discussions: Participate in industry forums, online communities, and events where your target audience is active and engage in discussions related to your book's topics. Pay attention to how your book is being mentioned or referenced in these conversations and the overall sentiment towards its ideas and insights.

By gathering this qualitative feedback, you can gain a more holistic understanding of your book's impact on your sales process and identify opportunities to refine your approach, update your content, or address any common concerns or misperceptions.

Measuring the impact of your book on your sales process is an ongoing and multi-faceted effort. By establishing key metrics and KPIs, analyzing your performance data, and gathering qualitative feedback from clients and sales team members, you can create a comprehensive picture of how your book is influencing your sales results and where it's delivering the most value. Use these insights to continually optimize your book-related sales strategies and maximize the ROI of your authorship investment.

Handling Prospects Who Have Already Read Your Book

When you encounter prospects who have already read your book, it presents a unique opportunity to deepen the relationship and demonstrate your value in a more targeted and personalized way.

These prospects have already invested time in exploring your ideas and insights, which indicates a higher level of interest and engagement than the average lead.

To effectively engage with prospects who are familiar with your book's content, consider the following strategies:

1. Ask for their key takeaways and favorite parts: Open the conversation by asking the prospect what stood out to them most from your book and which parts resonated with them on a personal or professional level. This shows that you value their perspective and are interested in understanding how your ideas have impacted them specifically.

2. Explore their specific challenges and goals: Use the prospect's familiarity with your book as a starting point to dive deeper into their unique situation and needs. Ask targeted questions about how the concepts from your book relate to their specific industry, role, or challenges, and invite them to share more about their goals and aspirations.

3. Provide personalized insights and recommendations: Based on the prospect's feedback, and the additional context they share, offer tailored insights and recommendations that build upon the foundational ideas from your book. Show how your book's strategies can be adapted or applied to their specific use case, and provide concrete examples or case studies that are relevant to their situation.

4. Invite them to a deeper discussion or workshop: If the prospect seems particularly engaged or interested in exploring your book's ideas further, invite them to a more in-depth discussion or workshop where you can dive into specific topics or exercises from your book. This could be a one-on-one session, or a small group workshop with other like-minded prospects.

5. Offer exclusive resources or bonuses: To reward the prospect's engagement and further demonstrate your value, consider offering exclusive resources or bonuses that are only available to readers of your book. This could include

templates, checklists, or additional case studies that build upon your book's content and help the prospect take action on your ideas.

By engaging with prospects who have already read your book in a thoughtful and personalized way, you can deepen the relationship, build trust, and demonstrate your unique value in addressing their specific needs and challenges.

Leveraging Their Familiarity to Dive Deeper into Specific Topics and Tailor Your Solutions

When prospects are already familiar with your book's content, it allows you to skip the basic introductions and jump straight into more advanced and nuanced conversations. This is an opportunity to showcase your deep expertise and thought leadership, and to position your offerings as the ideal solution for their specific needs.

To leverage the prospect's familiarity and tailor your solutions, consider the following approaches:

1. Explore their biggest takeaways and "aha" moments: Ask the prospect to share the most impactful insights or "aha" moments they experienced while reading your book. Use these as jumping-off points to explore the topics in greater depth, share additional examples or research, and discuss how these ideas can be applied to their specific industry or role.
2. Dive into their specific pain points and challenges: Use the prospect's familiarity with your book to have a more targeted conversation about the specific pain points or challenges they're facing. Ask probing questions to uncover the root causes and implications of these issues, and share how your book's strategies and your offerings can help address them in a customized way.
3. Provide a roadmap or action plan: Based on the prospect's unique goals and challenges, provide a personalized roadmap or action plan that outlines how they can implement your book's ideas and leverage your solutions for maximum im-

pact. Break down the steps into manageable phases, and offer specific metrics or milestones they can use to track their progress and ROI.

4. Share relevant case studies and success stories: To further demonstrate the value and applicability of your solutions, share case studies or success stories that are closely aligned with the prospect's situation. Highlight how other clients with similar challenges or goals have successfully implemented your book's strategies and achieved tangible results with your offerings.

5. Offer a customized proposal or solution: Based on the in-depth conversation and the specific needs and goals uncovered, develop a customized proposal or solution that is tailored to the prospect's unique requirements. Emphasize how your offerings build upon and extend the value of your book's ideas, and how they can help the prospect achieve their desired outcomes faster and more effectively.

By diving deeper into specific topics and tailoring your solutions to the prospect's unique needs, you can demonstrate your value as a strategic partner and trusted advisor, rather than just an author or vendor.

Using Your Book as a Springboard for More Advanced and Nuanced Conversations

When prospects have already read your book, it sets the stage for more advanced and nuanced conversations that go beyond the basics and demonstrate your deep expertise and thought leadership. By using your book as a springboard for these higher-level discussions, you can differentiate yourself from competitors and showcase the unique value you bring to the table.

To use your book as a springboard for more advanced conversations, consider the following strategies:

1. Explore the latest trends and developments: Use your book as a starting point to discuss the latest trends, research, or

developments in your industry that build upon or extend your book's ideas. Share your perspective on how these emerging topics impact your book's strategies and how your offerings are evolving to stay ahead of the curve.

2. Discuss potential future scenarios and implications: Engage the prospect in a forward-thinking discussion about potential future scenarios or implications related to your book's topics. Share your vision for how your ideas and solutions can help organizations navigate these future challenges and opportunities, and invite the prospect to share their own predictions and insights.

3. Address common misconceptions or objections: Use your book as a platform to address common misconceptions, objections, or pushback related to your ideas or solutions. Share examples or case studies that challenge these assumptions and demonstrate the real-world impact and value of your approach.

4. Explore adjacent or complementary topics: Identify adjacent or complementary topics that are related to your book's core ideas but not explicitly covered in the content. Use these as opportunities to showcase your broader expertise and thought leadership, and to discuss how your offerings can help organizations address these related challenges or opportunities.

5. Invite the prospect to co-create or beta test: If the prospect seems particularly engaged or aligned with your book's ideas, invite them to co-create or beta test new offerings or solutions that build upon your book's strategies. This could include participating in a pilot program, providing feedback on new content or tools, or collaborating on a case study or research project.

By using your book as a springboard for more advanced and nuanced conversations, you can position yourself as a cutting-edge thought leader and strategic partner who is always pushing the boundaries and exploring new possibilities. This can help you stand out in a crowded marketplace and build deeper, more valuable relationships with your prospects and clients.

Handling prospects who have already read your book requires a different approach than engaging with those who are new to your ideas. By leveraging their familiarity with your content, diving deeper into specific topics and challenges, and using your book as a springboard for more advanced conversations, you can demonstrate your unique value and expertise in a highly targeted and personalized way. This can help you build stronger relationships, close more deals, and establish yourself as a go-to resource and trusted advisor in your industry.

Chapter 6

Amplifying Your Book's Impact

Your book is more than just a powerful tool for establishing your authority and credibility; it can also serve as a springboard for securing lucrative speaking engagements. As a published author, you have already demonstrated your expertise and unique insights in your field, positioning you as a sought-after speaker for conferences, workshops, and corporate events.

The first step in leveraging your book for speaking engagements is to recognize the value you bring to the table. Your book showcases your deep understanding of your subject, your ability to communicate complex ideas effectively, and your capacity to captivate an audience with your words. These are all essential qualities that event organizers look for when selecting speakers.

To identify relevant speaking opportunities, start by researching conferences, trade shows, and industry events that align with your book's topic and target audience. Look for events that attract your ideal clients and have a track record of featuring high-caliber speakers. Don't be afraid to think outside the box, as your expertise may be valuable to audiences beyond your immediate niche.

Once you've identified potential speaking opportunities, craft a compelling pitch that highlights the unique value you can bring to the event. Use your book as a centerpiece of your pitch, emphasizing how your content can be adapted to deliver a powerful and engaging presentation. Share excerpts from your book that demonstrate your thought leadership and ability to captivate an audience.

When tailoring your book's content for speaking engagements, focus on the key insights and takeaways that will resonate most with your audience. Consider the specific challenges and goals of the event attendees and adapt your material accordingly. Use storytelling techniques to bring your ideas to life and create an emotional connection with your listeners.

In addition to keynote presentations, consider offering workshops or breakout sessions that dive deeper into the concepts covered in your book. These interactive formats allow you to engage with attendees on a more personal level, fostering meaningful connections and positioning yourself as a valuable resource.

As you secure speaking engagements, be sure to maximize the promotional opportunities they provide. Announce your speaking gigs on your website, social media channels, and email list, inviting your followers to attend or share the event with their networks. Collaborate with event organizers to cross-promote your appearance and leverage their marketing channels to expand your reach.

During your presentations, be sure to mention your book and offer attendees a special opportunity to purchase signed copies or access exclusive bonuses. This not only generates additional revenue but also helps to expand your book's impact and reach.

By leveraging your book for speaking engagements, you can amplify your message, connect with new audiences, and establish yourself as a true thought leader in your industry. Embrace the opportunities that your book provides and watch as your speaking career flourishes, driving significant growth for your business.

Using Your Book to Attract Media Attention

In today's competitive business landscape, gaining media attention and positive PR can be a game-changer for your brand. Fortunately, your book is a powerful tool that can help you establish your credibility, demonstrate your newsworthiness, and attract the interest of journalists and media outlets.

The first step in using your book to attract media attention is to recognize the inherent value it holds. By authoring a book, you have already positioned yourself as an expert in your field, with valuable insights and unique perspectives to share. This alone makes you a compelling candidate for interviews, expert commentary, and feature articles.

To capitalize on this opportunity, start by crafting a compelling press release that announces your book's launch and highlights its key themes and takeaways. Your press release should be concise, engaging, and clearly communicate the value your book brings to readers. Emphasize the unique insights and groundbreaking ideas that set your book apart from others in your industry.

When crafting your media pitch, focus on the specific angles and stories that will resonate with journalists and their audiences. Consider the current trends, challenges, and conversations happening in your industry, and position your book as a timely and relevant resource. Highlight the ways in which your book addresses these issues and offers fresh perspectives or practical solutions.

In addition to your book's launch, look for opportunities to tie your book's themes and insights to current events and news stories. For example, if your book focuses on leadership strategies, you could offer expert commentary on a high-profile leadership crisis in the news. By positioning yourself as a thought leader with valuable insights to share, you increase your chances of being featured in news articles and interviews.

When pitching to media outlets, be sure to tailor your approach to each specific journalist or publication. Research their previous coverage and identify the topics and angles that are most likely to capture their interest. Personalize your pitch, demonstrating that you understand their audience, and the unique value you can bring to their story.

As you secure media opportunities, be prepared to showcase your expertise and bring your book's ideas to life. Practice your talking points and develop engaging anecdotes and examples that illustrate your key messages. Remember that your goal is not simply to promote your book, but to provide value to the audience and establish yourself as a go-to resource in your field.

To maximize the impact of your media coverage, be sure to share your interviews, articles, and expert commentary across your own channels. Post links on your website, share on social media, and include highlights in your email newsletters. This not only expands the reach of your media coverage but also reinforces your credibility and authority to your existing audience.

By leveraging your book to attract media attention and PR, you can significantly amplify your message, reach new audiences, and establish yourself as a recognized expert in your industry. Embrace the power of your book and watch as it opens doors to exciting media opportunities, ultimately driving growth and success for your business.

Boosting Your Online Presence and SEO with Your Book

Having a strong online presence is essential for business success. Your book is a valuable asset that can help you boost your visibility, improve your search engine rankings, and drive targeted traffic to your website and online platforms.

The first step in optimizing your book for online success is to carefully craft its title, description, and metadata. Your book's title should be compelling, descriptive, and include relevant keywords that potential readers are likely to search for. Consider using a subtitle to provide additional context and incorporate key phrases that align with your book's content.

When writing your book's description, focus on creating a clear, concise, and engaging summary that showcases the unique value your book offers. Use persuasive language and highlight the key benefits readers will gain from your book. Be sure to naturally integrate relevant keywords throughout your description to improve its search engine visibility.

In addition to your book's title and description, pay close attention to its metadata. This includes elements such as your book's categories, tags, and author bio. Choose categories and tags that accurately reflect your book's content and target audience, making it easier for readers to discover your work. Craft an author bio that establishes your credibility and expertise, incorporating relevant keywords and phrases.

Beyond optimizing your book's online listing, leverage its content to create valuable blog posts, articles, and social media updates. Repurpose key insights, quotes, and excerpts from your book into engaging digital content that showcases your expertise and drives traffic back to your book and website.

When creating blog posts and articles based on your book, focus on providing actionable advice, thought-provoking ideas, and real-world examples that resonate with your target audience. Use compelling headlines and subheadings that incorporate relevant keywords, making it easier for readers to find your content through search engines.

On social media, share snippets from your book, along with your own commentary and insights. Engage with your followers by asking questions, sparking discussions, and encouraging them to share their own experiences related to your book's themes. Use relevant hashtags to expand your reach and make it easier for new audiences to discover your content.

To further drive traffic to your website and online platforms, consider offering exclusive bonuses or resources related to your book. This could include downloadable templates, worksheets, or additional chapters that complement your book's content. By providing valuable extras, you incentivize readers to visit your website and engage with your brand beyond the pages of your book.

Finally, leverage your book to build backlinks to your website. Reach out to bloggers, podcasters, and other influencers in your industry, offering to provide expert insights or contribute guest content based on your book's themes. By securing high-quality backlinks from reputable sources, you can improve your website's search engine rankings and drive targeted traffic to your online platforms.

By strategically leveraging your book to boost your online presence and SEO, you can amplify your reach, attract new audiences, and establish yourself as a thought leader in your industry. Embrace the power of digital marketing and watch as your book becomes a catalyst for online growth and success.

Leveraging Your Book for Strategic Partnerships and Joint Ventures

Your book is not only a powerful tool for establishing your authority and credibility but also a valuable asset for forging strategic partnerships and joint ventures. By aligning yourself with like-minded individuals and organizations, you can expand your reach, tap into new audiences, and create mutually beneficial opportunities for growth and success.

The first step in leveraging your book for strategic partnerships is to identify potential partners and collaborators who share your values, mission, and target audience. Look for individuals or organizations whose expertise and offerings complement your own, and whose audiences would benefit from the insights and ideas presented in your book.

When reaching out to potential partners, use your book as a powerful tool for initiating and nurturing these strategic relationships. Share a copy of your book with prospective collaborators, along with a personalized note highlighting the specific ways in which your book aligns with their work and how a partnership could be mutually beneficial.

Your book serves as a tangible demonstration of your expertise and thought leadership, making it easier to capture the attention and interest of potential partners. By providing value upfront and showcasing the quality of your ideas, you set the stage for productive conversations and collaboration opportunities.

As you engage with potential partners, explore ways to leverage your book as the centerpiece of co-marketing and co-branding initiatives. For example, consider hosting a joint webinar or workshop series that dives deeper into the themes and strategies presented in your book, with each partner bringing their unique perspectives and expertise to the table.

You could also explore opportunities for cross-promotion, such as featuring each other's books, products, or services in your respective email newsletters, social media channels, or websites. By tapping into each other's audiences and networks, you can expand your reach and attract new prospects who are likely to resonate with your message.

Another powerful way to leverage your book for strategic partnerships is to create co-branded resources or offerings that bundle your book with your partner's products or services. For example, if your book focuses on leadership development, you could partner with a company that offers executive coaching services to create a comprehensive leadership training program that includes your book as a core resource.

By bundling your book with complementary offerings, you create a unique and compelling value proposition that sets you apart from competitors and provides a seamless, integrated experience for your shared audience.

As you explore partnership and joint venture opportunities, be sure to clearly define the terms and expectations of each collaboration. Establish clear goals, roles, and responsibilities, and put agreements in place to protect both parties' interests and intellectual property.

Throughout the partnership process, maintain open and transparent communication with your collaborators, regularly sharing updates, insights, and feedback. By fostering strong, mutually beneficial relationships centered around your book, you lay the foundation for long-term success and growth.

Leveraging your book for strategic partnerships and joint ventures is a powerful way to amplify your impact, reach new audiences, and create exciting opportunities for growth and success. By aligning yourself with the right partners and collaborators, you can take your book—and your business—to new heights, achieving a level of success and influence that would be difficult to attain on your own.

Using Your Book to Expand Your Product or Service Offerings

Your book is more than just a standalone product; it's a powerful springboard for expanding your product or service offerings and creating new revenue streams. By leveraging the content, authority, and expertise showcased in your book, you can develop a range of complementary products and services that provide additional value to your audience and drive business growth.

One of the most effective ways to expand your offerings based on your book is to create online courses, workshops, or coaching programs that dive deeper into the concepts and strategies covered in your book. These offerings provide an opportunity for readers to engage with your ideas on a more interactive and personal level, while also allowing you to monetize your expertise beyond the pages of your book.

When developing these offerings, start by identifying the key themes, frameworks, and action steps from your book that lend themselves well to a more immersive learning experience. Consider the specific challenges, goals, and pain points of your target audience, and design your offerings to provide practical, actionable solutions that build upon the foundation laid in your book.

For example, if your book focuses on effective marketing strategies for small businesses, you could create an online course that walks participants through the process of developing and implementing a comprehensive marketing plan. Your course could include video lessons, downloadable templates, live Q&A sessions, and personalized feedback, providing a high-touch, value-packed experience that goes beyond the insights shared in your book.

Similarly, you could offer group coaching or mastermind programs that bring together readers who are looking to apply your book's principles to their specific businesses or challenges. These programs provide an opportunity for participants to learn from your expertise, as well as from the experiences and insights of their peers, creating a rich, collaborative learning environment.

In addition to courses and coaching programs, consider developing other complementary products or services that align with your book's content and audience. This could include workbooks, templates, or toolkits that help readers implement your ideas more effectively, or done-for-you services that provide personalized support and guidance based on your book's principles.

When launching and promoting these new offerings, leverage the authority and credibility established by your book. Use your book as a powerful marketing tool, highlighting excerpts or case studies that demonstrate the value and impact of your ideas. Offer special promotions or bonuses to your book's readers, rewarding their loyalty and encouraging them to take the next step in their journey with you.

You can also use your book to attract new audiences to your expanded offerings. Promote your courses, coaching programs, or other products and services through your book's website, social media channels, and email list, as well as through strategic partnerships and joint venture opportunities.

By leveraging your book as a platform for expanding your product or service offerings, you create a powerful ecosystem of value that supports your audience's growth and success while also driving your own business growth. As your readers engage with your complementary offerings and experience the transformative power of your ideas firsthand, they become loyal advocates for your brand, fueling word-of-mouth referrals and long-term success.

Using your book to expand your product or service offerings is a smart, strategic way to amplify your impact, create new revenue streams, and build a thriving, sustainable business. By providing your audience with multiple touchpoints and opportunities to engage with your expertise, you deepen your relationship with them and establish yourself as the go-to authority in your field.

Leveraging Your Book for Thought Leadership and Community Building

Writing a book is a powerful way to establish yourself as a thought leader in your industry. By sharing your unique insights, experiences, and perspectives, you demonstrate your expertise and set yourself apart as a leading voice in your field. However, thought leadership goes beyond simply publishing your ideas; it requires ongoing engagement, dialogue, and community building around your book's message.

To establish yourself as a thought leader, start by leveraging your book's content to spark meaningful conversations and discussions within your industry. Share excerpts, quotes, and key takeaways from your book across your social media channels, blog, and email list, inviting your audience to share their own thoughts and experiences related to your book's themes.

Engage with your readers by responding to their comments, questions, and feedback. Show genuine interest in their perspectives and use their insights to deepen your own understanding of your book's subject. By fostering a two-way dialogue with your audience, you demonstrate your commitment to ongoing learning and growth, while also building trust and rapport with your readers.

In addition to engaging with your audience online, look for opportunities to participate in industry events, conferences, and panels related to your book's topics. Share your insights and ideas from the stage, and use your book as a jumping-off point for deeper discussions and collaborations with other thought leaders in your field.

As you engage with your audience and establish yourself as a thought leader, focus on building a loyal community around your book's message. This community can serve as a powerful source of support, inspiration, and ongoing growth for both you and your readers.

To foster a sense of community around your book, consider creating a dedicated online space where readers can connect with each other and engage in ongoing discussions related to your book's themes. This could be a private Facebook group, a LinkedIn community, or a forum on your own website.

Within this community, encourage readers to share their own experiences, challenges, and successes related to your book's ideas. Facilitate discussions and prompt conversations that help readers apply your book's insights to their own lives and businesses. By creating a space for your readers to connect and support each other, you deepen their engagement with your message and create a sense of belonging and shared purpose.

To keep your community engaged and thriving, regularly share new content, resources, and opportunities that align with your book's themes. This could include blog posts, podcasts, webinars, or live Q&A sessions that provide additional value and support to your readers.

You can also use your community as a source of valuable feedback and insights for your own thought leadership and business growth. Regularly seek input from your readers on the challenges they're facing, the topics they'd like to see you address, and the ways in which your ideas have impacted their lives and work. Use this feedback to refine your messaging, develop new products or services, and stay attuned to the evolving needs and interests of your audience.

By leveraging your book for thought leadership and community building, you create a powerful platform for ongoing impact and influence. As your ideas spread, and your community grows, you establish yourself as a trusted authority and valued resource in your industry, opening up new opportunities for growth, collaboration, and success.

Ultimately, thought leadership and community building are about more than just promoting your book or building your brand; they're about making a meaningful difference in the lives and work of others. By sharing your insights, engaging with your readers, and fostering a sense of connection and shared purpose, you create a ripple effect of positive change that extends far beyond the pages of your book.

Part 3: Real-World Examples and Action Steps

Chapter 7

Case Studies of Businesses That Have Used This Strategy

As professional ghostwriters, we have the privilege of collaborating with a diverse array of clients from various industries and backgrounds. While the following case studies illustrate powerful examples of how books can drive business breakthroughs, we have taken measures to protect our clients' privacy by anonymizing or creating composite examples. The stories you'll read are inspired by real experiences, but with any identifying details obscured or fictionalized. This allows us to share valuable insights while maintaining the confidentiality that is paramount in our line of work. Although the names, locations, and certain specifics may be altered, the core principles and strategies highlighted remain universally applicable and transformative for entrepreneurs, thought leaders, and professionals seeking to leverage books for business growth.

Case Study 1: The Consultant's Handbook

Meet Sarah Thompson, a management consultant with over a decade of experience helping businesses improve their operations and boost their bottom line. Despite her impressive track record and glowing client testimonials, Sarah found herself struggling to stand out in an increasingly competitive market. She knew she had the expertise and insights to make a real difference for her clients, but needed a way to differentiate herself and attract higher-quality leads.

That's when Sarah decided to write "The Consultant's Handbook: Proven Strategies for Transforming Your Clients' Businesses." She collaborated with a skilled ghostwriter to capture her unique methodology and case studies, focusing on providing actionable advice and practical tools that readers could immediately implement in their own consulting practices.

Key strategies Sarah employed in writing and leveraging her book included:

1. Positioning the book as a comprehensive guide for both new and experienced consultants, covering topics such as client acquisition, project management, and delivering measurable results.
2. Incorporating real-world examples and case studies from her own consulting engagements to demonstrate the effectiveness of her approach and build credibility.
3. Offering valuable templates, checklists, and worksheets as downloadable resources to accompany the book, providing readers with practical tools they could use in their own work.
4. Leveraging the book to secure speaking engagements and workshops at industry conferences and events, further establishing her authority and reaching new audiences.
5. Integrating the book into her sales process, using it as a powerful lead magnet and follow-up tool to nurture prospects and convert them into clients.

The impact of "The Consultant's Handbook" on Sarah's business was transformative. Within months of the book's release, she saw a significant increase in qualified leads and new client inquiries. The book helped her attract larger, more sophisticated clients who were willing to invest in her premium consulting services.

By positioning herself as a published authority, Sarah was able to command higher fees and secure long-term retainer agreements with several prestigious organizations. The book also opened doors to new opportunities, such as keynote speaking invitations and strategic partnerships with complementary service providers.

Perhaps most importantly, "The Consultant's Handbook" allowed Sarah to make a more meaningful impact on her clients' businesses. By sharing her proven strategies and frameworks, she empowered readers to achieve better results and become more effective consultants in their own right.

Sarah's success story illustrates the incredible potential of writing a book to accelerate business growth and establish oneself as a true expert in their field. By providing tangible value and leveraging her book strategically, Sarah was able to transform her consulting practice and achieve a new level of professional success and fulfillment.

Case Study 2: The Fitness Entrepreneur's Guide

Jason Lee had always been passionate about fitness and helping others achieve their health goals. As a personal trainer and gym owner, he had built a successful business, but felt limited by the number of clients he could serve directly. Jason knew he had valuable knowledge and experience to share with a wider audience, particularly aspiring fitness entrepreneurs looking to start and grow their own businesses.

Motivated by a desire to make a bigger impact and leave a lasting legacy, Jason decided to write "The Fitness Entrepreneur's Guide: Building a Thriving Business in the Health and Wellness Industry." He teamed up with a ghostwriter who specializes in the fitness niche to help him articulate his unique perspective and create a compelling, actionable book.

Jason's content strategy focused on several key areas:

1. Sharing his personal story of overcoming challenges and building a successful fitness business from the ground up, to inspire and relate to readers on a human level.
2. Providing practical advice and step-by-step guidance on topics such as defining a target market, developing a unique brand, creating profitable service offerings, and implementing effective marketing strategies.
3. Addressing common mistakes and pitfalls that new fitness entrepreneurs often face, and offering proven solutions and workarounds based on Jason's own experience.
4. Incorporating case studies and success stories from other thriving fitness businesses to illustrate key concepts and provide real-world examples of the book's principles in action.

The book's unique value proposition lay in its combination of Jason's personal insights, industry-specific guidance, and a holistic approach to building a sustainable fitness business. Rather than focusing solely on the technical aspects of training or the latest workout trends, "The Fitness Entrepreneur's Guide" took a comprehensive view of what it takes to succeed as a health and wellness professional in today's competitive market.

Upon releasing the book, Jason saw a surge in interest and engagement from both existing and new audiences. Some tangible outcomes and success metrics included:

1. A 150% increase in email subscribers and social media followers within the first 3 months of the book's launch, as readers sought to connect with Jason and learn more about his approach.
2. Dozens of glowing reviews and testimonials from readers who found the book invaluable in starting or growing their own fitness businesses, with many citing specific strategies or insights that directly contributed to their success.
3. A significant uptick in inquiries for Jason's consulting and coaching services, as readers sought to work with him di-

rectly to implement the book's principles in their own businesses.

4. Invitations to speak at major fitness industry conferences and events, positioning Jason as a sought-after expert and thought leader in the entrepreneurial space.

5. The launch of a successful online course and mastermind group based on the book's content, providing an additional revenue stream and allowing Jason to support aspiring fitness entrepreneurs on a larger scale.

Perhaps most gratifyingly, Jason received countless messages from readers sharing how "The Fitness Entrepreneur's Guide" had not only transformed their businesses, but also their lives. Many expressed gratitude for the newfound clarity, confidence, and sense of purpose they had gained from reading the book and applying its lessons.

For Jason, the book's success was a testament to the power of sharing one's knowledge and experience to make a positive impact on others. By leveraging his book as a platform to educate, inspire, and empower fellow fitness entrepreneurs, he had not only accelerated his own business growth, but also helped shape the future of the industry he loved.

Case Study 3: The Tech Startup's Playbook

Samantha Patel, the founder and CEO of a fast-growing software-as-a-service (SaaS) startup, operated in a fiercely competitive and rapidly evolving industry. Her company offered innovative project management solutions for remote teams, but struggled to differentiate itself from the myriad of similar tools on the market. Samantha knew that to stand out and capture a larger share of the market, she needed to establish her startup as a thought leader and trusted resource in the realm of remote work and collaboration.

To achieve this goal, Samantha wrote "The Tech Startup's Playbook: Secrets to Scaling Your Remote Team and Thriving in the Digital

Age." The book was a distillation of her hard-won insights and experiences building a successful SaaS business, as well as a practical guide for entrepreneurs navigating the challenges of managing and growing a remote team.

Samantha took an innovative approach to integrating the book into her startup's marketing and sales efforts. Some key strategies included:

1. Offering the book as a free download on the company's website in exchange for users' email addresses, allowing the startup to build a targeted list of potential customers interested in remote work solutions.
2. Creating a series of webinars and online workshops based on the book's content, providing value to potential customers while subtly showcasing the startup's expertise and product offerings.
3. Leveraging the book to secure media coverage and podcast interviews, increasing the startup's visibility and credibility in the industry.
4. Integrating the book's frameworks and case studies into the startup's sales process, using them to educate prospects and demonstrate the value of the company's solutions.
5. Launching a branded online community for remote work leaders and entrepreneurs, using the book as a foundational resource and discussion starter to foster engagement and build relationships with potential customers.

The impact of "The Tech Startup's Playbook" on Samantha's business was significant and measurable. Some key outcomes included:

1. A 200% increase in qualified leads generated through the book's download landing page within the first 6 months of launch.
2. A 30% increase in free trial sign-ups for the startup's project management software, attributed to the increased visibility and credibility gained through the book and related marketing efforts.

3. A 15% higher conversion rate from free trial to paid sub-scription, as users who had engaged with the book's content and webinars were more likely to recognize the value of the startup's solutions.
4. A dramatic increase in media coverage and backlinks to the startup's website, improving its search engine rankings and organic traffic.
5. Multiple invitations for Samantha to speak at industry con-ferences and events as an expert on remote team manage-ment and SaaS growth strategies.

Beyond these quantitative metrics, "The Tech Startup's Playbook" also had a profound impact on the startup's brand authority and market positioning. By sharing her knowledge and experiences transparently and generously, Samantha established herself, and her company as trusted allies and resources for entrepreneurs navigat-ing the challenges of building and scaling remote teams.

The book helped to humanize the startup and create a deeper emo-tional connection with its target audience, fostering a sense of com-munity and loyalty that extended far beyond any single product or feature. Customers who had read the book felt that they were not just buying a software solution, but partnering with a company that truly understood their needs and was invested in their success.

For Samantha and her team, "The Tech Startup's Playbook" was a powerful demonstration of the value of thought leadership and con-tent marketing in driving business growth. By leveraging the book strategically across multiple channels and touchpoints, they were able to attract, engage, and convert customers more effectively than ever before, while also building a strong foundation for long-term brand equity and customer loyalty.

Case Study 4: The Non-Profit Leader's Memoir

For over two decades, Michael Thompson had been a tireless advo-cate for affordable housing and community development. As the founder and executive director of a non-profit organization dedicated to helping low-income families achieve homeownership, Michael had witnessed firsthand the transformative power of stable housing in breaking the cycle of poverty.

However, despite his organization's many successes, Michael felt that the wider public still lacked a deep understanding of the issues faced by the families his non-profit served. He believed that by sharing his personal journey, and the stories of those he had helped, he could inspire greater empathy, engagement, and support for the cause of affordable housing.

With this purpose in mind, Michael wrote "Building Hope: One Man's Journey to Empower Communities and Transform Lives." The memoir wove together Michael's own narrative of growing up in poverty and finding his calling as a community advocate with the stories of the families and individuals his organization had assisted over the years.

To leverage the memoir for maximum impact, Michael and his team implemented several key strategies:

1. Launching a "Building Hope" book tour, with author events and signings at bookstores, community centers, and libraries in the cities where the non-profit operated.
2. Partnering with local media outlets to secure interviews and feature stories about the book and the non-profit's mission, raising awareness among a wider audience.
3. Integrating the book into the non-profit's donor outreach and fundraising efforts, offering signed copies as premiums for new and recurring donations.
4. Creating a discussion guide and toolkit for community groups and book clubs to facilitate conversations and action around affordable housing issues.
5. Leveraging the book to forge new partnerships with like-minded organizations, foundations, and corporate sponsors committed to supporting the cause.

The impact of "Building Hope" on Michael's non-profit and the wider affordable housing movement was profound. Some key outcomes included:

1. A 75% increase in individual donations in the year following the book's release, as readers were inspired to contribute to the non-profit's mission.
2. The recruitment of dozens of new volunteers and board members who had learned about the organization through the book and felt compelled to get involved.
3. Increased media coverage and public discourse around affordable housing issues, with the book serving as a catalyst for deeper conversations and policy debates.
4. The formation of new strategic partnerships with major corporations, foundations, and government agencies, leading to expanded funding and resources for the non-profit's programs.
5. A measurable uptick in community engagement and grassroots advocacy efforts, as readers of the book felt empowered to take action and make a difference in their own communities.

Beyond these tangible outcomes, "Building Hope" also had a profound emotional impact on readers, humanizing the issue of affordable housing and fostering a greater sense of empathy and connection. Many readers reached out to Michael and his team to share their own stories and express gratitude for the work the non-profit was doing.

For Michael, the success of the memoir was a testament to the power of storytelling to inspire change and mobilize support for a cause. By sharing his own journey and the experiences of those his organization had helped, he was able to touch hearts, change minds, and build a stronger, more engaged community of advocates and supporters.

The "Building Hope" case study demonstrates how a non-profit leader's memoir can be a powerful tool for raising awareness, generating support, and driving meaningful impact. By leveraging the book strategically and integrating it into the organization's mission and outreach efforts, Michael and his team were able to achieve remarkable outcomes and accelerate their work in creating a more just and equitable society.

Case Study 5: The Artist's Business Breakthrough

Emily Chen, a talented visual artist, had spent years honing her craft and developing a distinctive style that blended traditional Chinese brush painting techniques with contemporary digital media. Despite critical acclaim and a growing following on social media, Emily struggled to translate her artistic passion into a sustainable business. She found it challenging to price her work, negotiate with galleries, and attract consistent commissions.

Determined to take control of her career and build a thriving art business, Emily decided to write "The Artist's Business Breakthrough: Strategies for Turning Your Creative Passion into a Profitable Career." The book was a unique fusion of Emily's personal journey as an artist, practical business advice tailored to the art world, and insights into the creative process that could help other artists overcome their own challenges.

Emily's goals in writing the book were twofold: to establish herself as a thought leader and mentor in the art community, and to attract higher-quality clients and opportunities that aligned with her values and artistic vision.

To achieve these goals, Emily employed several creative tactics:

1. Designing a visually stunning book cover and interior layout that showcased her artistic style and set the book apart from typical business titles.
2. Collaborating with other artists and influencers to create a series of video interviews and behind-the-scenes studio

tours that complemented the book's content and provided additional value to readers.

3. Launching a "Business Breakthrough" challenge on social media, encouraging artists to read the book and implement its strategies, then share their progress and successes using a dedicated hashtag.

4. Hosting a virtual book launch event that doubled as an online art exhibition, featuring Emily's work alongside that of other artists who had inspired or been influenced by her.

5. Creating a series of limited-edition prints and merchandise featuring artwork from the book, providing readers with a tangible connection to Emily's creative vision.

The impact of "The Artist's Business Breakthrough" on Emily's career was significant and wide-ranging. Some tangible results included:

1. A 200% increase in commissioned work in the six months following the book's release, as readers and collectors gained a deeper appreciation for Emily's artistic process and value.

2. Invitations to participate in several high-profile group exhibitions and solo shows, as gallery owners and curators discovered Emily's work through the book and associated media coverage.

3. A significant increase in licensing and collaboration opportunities, as brands and fellow artists sought to partner with Emily based on her unique style and business acumen.

4. The successful launch of Emily's own online art academy, teaching the principles and strategies from the book to aspiring artists around the world.

5. A more confident and empowered approach to pricing, negotiations, and client relationships, as Emily implemented the advice from her own book and saw firsthand the positive results.

Beyond these measurable outcomes, "The Artist's Business Breakthrough" also had a profound impact on Emily's personal brand and reputation within the art world. By sharing her knowledge and experiences openly and generously, she became a trusted resource and role model for other artists seeking to build sustainable careers.

The book also helped to spark important conversations and collaborations within the art community, as readers connected with each other and shared their own insights and challenges. Emily found herself at the center of a growing movement of artists who were passionate about not only creating meaningful work, but also building thriving businesses that could support and sustain their creative visions.

For Emily, the success of "The Artist's Business Breakthrough" was a powerful validation of her experiences and expertise, and a testament to the transformative power of combining creativity with strategic business thinking. By leveraging her book to build her brand, attract aligned clients, and empower fellow artists, she had not only achieved her own career goals, but also made a lasting impact on the art world as a whole.

Analyzing the Common Threads of Success

Throughout these five case studies, we've seen compelling examples of how professionals from diverse industries have leveraged books to achieve remarkable business breakthroughs. While each story is unique, there are several common threads that contribute to their success and offer valuable lessons for readers looking to apply these strategies to their own ventures.

One of the key factors that stands out across all five case studies is the power of strategic positioning. Whether it's Sarah establishing herself as the go-to expert for consultants, Jason becoming a trusted resource for fitness entrepreneurs, or Emily empowering fellow artists to build thriving businesses, each author used their book to carve out a distinct niche and establish their authority within their respective fields. By identifying a specific target audience and tailoring their book's content to address the unique challenges and aspirations of that group, these authors were able to create a powerful resonance and connection with their readers.

Another critical element of success that emerges from these case studies is the importance of leveraging the book across multiple channels and touchpoints. From Michael's "Building Hope" book tour and community partnerships to Samantha's webinars and online community, each author found creative ways to integrate their book into their broader marketing and outreach efforts. By treating the book not as an isolated project, but as a versatile tool that could be adapted and applied in various contexts, these authors were able to maximize its impact and reach.

A third key factor that contributes to the success of these case studies is the focus on providing tangible value and practical insights to readers. Whether it's Jason's step-by-step guidance for building a successful fitness business, Emily's strategies for navigating the art world, or Sarah's templates and checklists for consultants, each book goes beyond theoretical advice to offer concrete, actionable takeaways that readers can implement in their own lives and work. By prioritizing the reader's needs and delivering real-world solutions, these authors were able to create a lasting impact and cultivate a loyal following.

Beyond these specific strategies, the case studies also highlight some universal principles that can be applied across industries and business models. One such principle is the power of authenticity and vulnerability in creating a deep emotional connection with readers. By sharing their personal stories, challenges, and triumphs, authors like Michael and Emily were able to humanize their expertise and foster a sense of trust and relatability with their audience.

Another overarching lesson is the importance of a clear and compelling purpose behind the book. Whether it's Sarah's desire to make a bigger impact on the consulting industry, Samantha's mission to empower remote teams, or Michael's commitment to affordable housing, each author's book was driven by a strong "why" that informed every aspect of its creation and promotion. By aligning their book with a larger vision and set of values, these authors were able to create a sense of meaning and momentum that extended far beyond the page.

Perhaps the most inspiring takeaway from these case studies is the sheer versatility and adaptability of the book as a tool for business growth. From tech startups to non-profits, fitness studios to art galleries, these stories demonstrate that the power of a well-crafted book transcends any single industry or niche. By tapping into the universal human desires for knowledge, connection, and transformation, a book has the potential to create breakthrough results in virtually any field.

As readers reflect on these case studies and extract lessons for their own ventures, it's important to remember that the specific tactics and approaches may vary depending on one's unique context and goals. However, by embracing the underlying principles of strategic positioning, multichannel integration, tangible value creation, authenticity, purpose alignment, and versatility, aspiring authors across industries can harness the transformative potential of a book to achieve their own business breakthroughs.

Ultimately, these case studies serve as a powerful testament to the enduring impact and influence of the written word. By sharing their stories, insights, and expertise through the medium of a book, these authors have not only achieved remarkable results for their own businesses, but also inspired and empowered countless others to do the same. As readers embark on their own book-writing journeys, they can draw strength and guidance from the examples of those who have gone before them, while also forging their own unique paths to success.

Chapter 8

Your Action Plan for Leveraging Your Book

As you embark on your journey to leverage your book for business growth, it's crucial to take a step back and revisit the core purpose and goals behind your book project. This introspective process will serve as the foundation for your action plan, ensuring that every step you take is aligned with your overarching objectives.

First, clarify your primary objectives for writing and leveraging your book. Are you aiming to establish yourself as a thought leader in your industry, attract high-quality clients, or generate leads for your products or services? Perhaps you want to open doors to speaking engagements, media opportunities, or strategic partnerships. Whatever your specific goals may be, it's essential to articulate them clearly and keep them at the forefront of your mind throughout the book-writing and promotion process.

Next, consider how your book's purpose aligns with your overall business goals. Your book should not be a standalone project, but rather an integral part of your broader business strategy. Reflect on how your book can support and amplify your existing products, services, and brand messaging. For example, if your business focuses on providing innovative solutions to a specific problem, your book should showcase your expertise in that area and demonstrate how your approach stands out from competitors.

To ensure that your book delivers tangible results, it's important to define specific, measurable targets for your book's impact and success. These targets should be directly tied to your primary objectives and business goals. For instance, if your goal is to attract new clients, set a target for the number of leads or client inquiries generated through your book. If you aim to secure speaking engagements, define a target for the number of invitations or bookings you want to achieve within a specific timeframe.

When setting these targets, be ambitious but realistic. Consider your current resources, platform, and network, and assess what's achievable given your starting point. Keep in mind that your book's success is not solely measured by sales figures or bestseller rankings, but rather by its ability to drive meaningful results for your business.

By revisiting your book's purpose and goals, you lay the groundwork for a focused and effective action plan. With clarity around your objectives, alignment with your business strategy, and specific targets to strive for, you'll be well-equipped to navigate the exciting journey ahead and leverage your book for transformative business growth.

Assessing Your Current Situation and Resources

Before diving into the book-writing process, it's essential to take stock of your current situation and resources. This self-assessment will help you identify your strengths, pinpoint potential challenges, and develop a realistic plan for bringing your book to life.

Start by evaluating your existing platform, network, and resources. Consider the following questions:

1. What is your current level of visibility and influence within your industry?

2. How engaged and supportive is your existing audience or customer base?
3. What relevant connections or partnerships do you have that could support your book's promotion and distribution?
4. What skills, knowledge, and experience do you bring to the table that will contribute to your book's success?
5. What financial and time resources can you realistically allocate to your book project?

Answering these questions honestly will give you a clearer picture of your starting point, and the assets you can leverage throughout your book-writing journey.

Next, identify potential gaps or challenges that may arise during the book-writing process. These could include:

1. Limited writing experience or confidence in your ability to communicate your ideas effectively
2. Time constraints due to existing business commitments and responsibilities
3. Lack of a strong online presence or engaged audience to promote your book
4. Financial limitations that may impact your ability to invest in professional editing, design, or marketing services

By anticipating these challenges early on, you can proactively develop strategies to overcome them. For example, if writing is not your strong suit, you may consider working with a ghostwriter or collaborating with a co-author. If time is a concern, you may need to block out dedicated writing sessions in your calendar or delegate some business tasks to free up space for your book project.

Finally, develop a realistic timeline and budget for your book project. Your timeline should take into account the various stages of the book-writing process, including:

1. Planning and outlining your book's content
2. Conducting research and gathering supporting materials
3. Drafting and revising your manuscript

4. Editing and proofreading your book
5. Designing your book's cover and interior layout
6. Developing and executing your book launch and promotion plan

Be sure to allocate sufficient time for each stage, factoring in any potential delays or setbacks. It's better to overestimate the time you'll need than to rush the process and compromise the quality of your book.

Your budget should account for any professional services or resources you'll need to bring your book to life, such as:

1. Ghostwriting or editing services
2. Cover design and interior layout
3. ISBN and copyright registration
4. Printing and distribution costs
5. Marketing and promotion expenses

Be realistic about what you can afford to invest in your book project, and prioritize the expenses that will have the greatest impact on your book's success. Keep in mind that your book is a long-term investment in your business, and the resources you dedicate to it now can pay off in significant ways down the line.

By assessing your current situation and resources, identifying potential challenges, and developing a realistic timeline and budget, you'll be well-prepared to navigate the book-writing journey with confidence and clarity. This foundation will set you up for success as you take the next steps toward leveraging your book for business growth.

Developing Your Book Content Strategy

With a clear understanding of your book's purpose and a solid grasp of your resources, it's time to dive into the heart of your book project: developing your content strategy. This crucial step will shape the direction and impact of your book, ensuring that it resonates with your target audience and achieves your desired outcomes.

Start by determining your book's core theme, message, and unique value proposition. Your core theme should encapsulate the overarching topic or subject of your book, while your message should convey the key takeaways or lessons you want your readers to glean from your content. Your unique value proposition should highlight what sets your book apart from others in your industry or niche. Consider the following questions:

1. What specific problem or challenge does your book aim to solve for your readers?
2. What unique insights, strategies, or perspectives do you bring to the table?
3. How does your book's content align with your business's mission and values?
4. What transformative outcomes can your readers expect from implementing your book's ideas?

Crafting a clear and compelling core theme, message, and unique value proposition will serve as the guiding light for your content creation process, ensuring that every chapter and paragraph stays true to your book's central purpose.

Next, outline your book's structure and key content areas. A well-organized outline will serve as the backbone of your book, providing a clear roadmap for your writing journey. Start by breaking down your book into main sections or parts, each focusing on a specific aspect of your overarching theme. Within each section, identify the key chapters or subtopics you'll need to cover to fully explore your ideas.

As you outline your content, consider the logical flow and progression of your ideas. Each chapter should build upon the previous one, leading your readers on a cohesive journey from beginning to end. Use storytelling techniques, real-world examples, and practical insights to illustrate your points and keep your readers engaged.

To ensure that your book's content is comprehensive, accurate, and valuable to your readers, it's important to develop effective strategies for researching, organizing, and refining your material. This may involve:

1. Conducting interviews with industry experts or thought leaders
2. Gathering case studies and success stories from your own business or clients
3. Reviewing relevant literature, research, and data to support your ideas
4. Seeking feedback from beta readers or a focus group to validate your content's relevance and impact

As you research and gather information, use a system to organize your findings, such as a digital notebook, spreadsheet, or project management tool. This will help you keep track of your sources, ideas, and progress, and make it easier to integrate your research into your writing.

Finally, as you draft your chapters, be sure to build in time for revising and refining your content. This may involve multiple rounds of editing to ensure that your ideas are clear, concise, and compelling. Consider working with a professional editor or writing coach to provide objective feedback and help you polish your manuscript to perfection.

By developing a strong book content strategy, you'll lay the foundation for a powerful and impactful book that not only showcases your expertise but also drives meaningful results for your business. With a clear theme, message, and structure in place, you'll be well-equipped to craft a book that resonates with your target audience and positions you as a true authority in your field.

Choosing the Right Ghostwriting and Publishing Path

With your book content strategy in place, it's time to consider the various options available for bringing your book to life. One of the most critical decisions you'll make is choosing the right ghostwriting and publishing path. This decision will have a significant impact on the quality, timeline, and overall success of your book project.

When it comes to ghostwriting, it's essential to understand the different options available and select a ghostwriter who aligns with your needs, goals, and vision. A skilled ghostwriter can help you transform your ideas and expertise into a compelling, well-structured book that captures your unique voice and resonates with your target audience.

To find the right ghostwriter for your project, start by assessing their unique qualifications and expertise. Look for a ghostwriter who has:

1. A strong writing background and a proven track record of success in your industry or niche
2. A deep understanding of your subject and the ability to convey complex ideas in an engaging, accessible way
3. A writing style that aligns with your brand voice and resonates with your target audience
4. Positive testimonials and case studies from previous clients that demonstrate their ability to deliver high-quality work

When evaluating potential ghostwriters, take the time to review their portfolios, read samples of their work, and speak with them directly to get a sense of their communication style and approach to collaboration.

In addition to their writing skills and expertise, it's also important to consider a ghostwriter's track record and client successes. Look for a ghostwriter who has helped their clients achieve notable results, such as:

1. Increased visibility and credibility within their industry

2. Higher-quality leads and client acquisitions
3. Expanded opportunities for speaking engagements, media appearances, and strategic partnerships
4. Improved brand recognition and thought leadership positioning

By reviewing case studies and success stories from a ghostwriter's previous clients, you can gain valuable insights into the specific results and impact they have achieved and determine whether they are the right fit for your project.

Finally, when choosing a ghostwriter, it's crucial to understand their specific approach and process. Look for a ghostwriter who:

1. Has a clear, structured process for collaborating with clients and bringing their book projects to life
2. Communicates openly and regularly throughout the writing process, providing updates and opportunities for feedback and input
3. Uses proven project management tools and techniques to keep your book on track and ensure timely delivery
4. Has rigorous quality control measures in place to ensure that your book meets the highest standards of excellence

By gaining insight into a ghostwriter's collaborative process and project management approach, you can ensure that your book project runs smoothly and efficiently from start to finish.

When it comes to publishing your book, there are several options to consider, including traditional publishing, self-publishing, and hybrid publishing. Each path has its own advantages and considerations, and the right choice will depend on your specific goals, resources, and timeline.

Traditional publishing involves working with a well-established publishing house to produce and distribute your book. While this path can offer prestige and wide distribution, it also typically involves a longer timeline and less control over the final product.

Self-publishing, on the other hand, gives you complete control over your book's content, design, and distribution, but requires a significant investment of time and resources on your part.

Hybrid publishing offers a middle ground, combining elements of both traditional and self-publishing. With this approach, you typically pay for certain services, such as editing and distribution, while retaining greater control over your book's content and timeline.

By carefully considering your options and selecting the ghostwriting and publishing path that aligns with your goals and resources, you can set your book up for success and maximize its impact on your business. With the right team and approach in place, you'll be well on your way to creating a powerful, impactful book that drives real results for your brand and your bottom line.

Crafting Your Book Promotion and Distribution Plan

With your book written and ready to be shared with the world, it's time to shift your focus to promotion and distribution. A well-crafted book promotion and distribution plan is essential for ensuring that your book reaches your target audience and achieves your desired impact.

To begin, develop a multichannel marketing strategy that leverages a variety of tactics and platforms to promote your book. This may include:

1. Social media marketing: Utilize your existing social media presence to build buzz around your book, share teasers and excerpts, and engage with your followers.
2. Email marketing: Leverage your email list to announce your book launch, share behind-the-scenes content, and offer exclusive bonuses or incentives for purchasing your book.
3. Content marketing: Create valuable, informative content related to your book's themes and share it on your blog, web-

site, and other relevant platforms to attract potential readers and build anticipation for your book.

4. Paid advertising: Consider investing in targeted advertising on platforms like Facebook, Instagram, or Amazon to reach new audiences and drive book sales.
5. Influencer outreach: Identify influencers and thought leaders in your industry who may be interested in reading and promoting your book to their followers.
6. Media outreach: Pitch your book to relevant media outlets, including podcasts, blogs, and publications, to secure interviews, reviews, and feature articles.

As you develop your marketing strategy, be sure to identify key promotional activities and partnerships that can help amplify your book's reach. This may include:

1. Book launch events: Host a virtual or in-person book launch event to generate excitement and drive initial sales.
2. Speaking engagements: Seek out opportunities to speak at conferences, workshops, or webinars related to your book's themes, and use these platforms to promote your book and establish your thought leadership.
3. Partnerships with complementary businesses: Identify businesses or organizations that serve a similar target audience and explore opportunities for cross-promotion or collaboration.
4. Giveaways and contests: Run a giveaway or contest to incentivize people to engage with your book and share it with their networks.
5. Bundling and upselling: Offer your book as part of a bundle or package with your other products or services to increase its perceived value and drive sales.

In addition to your promotional efforts, it's crucial to create a distribution plan that ensures your book reaches your target audience. This may involve:

1. Choosing the right distribution channels: Determine which online and offline distribution channels are most relevant to your target audience, such as Amazon, Barnes & Noble, or independent bookstores.
2. Optimizing your book listing: Ensure that your book's listing on each distribution platform is optimized with compelling copy, keywords, and categories to improve its discoverability and attract potential readers.
3. Leveraging print-on-demand technology: Consider using print-on-demand services to minimize upfront costs and ensure that your book is always available for purchase.
4. Offering multiple formats: Make your book available in multiple formats, such as e-book, paperback, and audiobook, to cater to different reader preferences and maximize your reach.
5. Exploring international distribution: If your book has global appeal, consider partnering with international distributors or making your book available in multiple languages to reach readers around the world.

By crafting a comprehensive book promotion and distribution plan, you can ensure that your book gains maximum visibility and reaches the right readers at the right time. Remember, promoting your book is an ongoing process that requires consistent effort and attention. By staying committed to your promotional efforts and continually seeking out new opportunities to share your book with the world, you can achieve long-term success and establish yourself as a true thought leader in your industry.

Integrating Your Book into Your Overall Business Strategy

Writing and publishing a book is a significant achievement, but to truly maximize its impact, it's essential to integrate your book into your overall business strategy. By aligning your book with your broader business objectives and leveraging it as a strategic asset, you can create a powerful synergy that drives long-term success.

To begin, take the time to map out how your book aligns with and supports your overarching business goals. Consider questions such as:

1. How does your book's content reinforce your brand messaging and values?
2. How can your book help you attract and engage your ideal clients or customers?
3. How can your book differentiate you from competitors and establish your unique value proposition?
4. How can your book support your business's growth and expansion plans?

By clearly defining the ways in which your book aligns with your business objectives, you can ensure that your book is not just a one-time project, but a strategic tool that supports your long-term success.

Next, identify specific opportunities to integrate your book into your existing products, services, and client interactions. This may involve:

1. Incorporating your book into your sales and marketing materials, such as your website, brochures, and proposals
2. Using your book as a lead generation tool, offering a free chapter or excerpt in exchange for email sign-ups or contact information
3. Giving your book as a gift to new clients or customers as a way to welcome them and provide additional value
4. Referencing your book in your consulting or coaching sessions, using it as a tool to reinforce key concepts and strategies
5. Creating companion resources, such as workbooks, templates, or online courses, that align with your book's content and provide additional value to readers

By integrating your book into your existing offerings and interactions, you can create a cohesive and memorable experience for your clients and customers, reinforcing your expertise and value at every touchpoint.

Finally, develop a long-term plan for leveraging your book as a strategic asset. This may involve:

1. Continuously promoting your book through your marketing and communication channels, even after the initial launch period

2. Seeking out opportunities to speak, write, or consult on topics related to your book, positioning yourself as a go-to expert in your field

3. Using your book as a springboard to develop new products, services, or programs that expand upon its key themes and ideas

4. Regularly updating and refreshing your book's content to ensure that it remains relevant and valuable to your target audience

5. Exploring opportunities to license or repurpose your book's content for other formats or platforms, such as podcasts, video series, or online courses

By developing a long-term plan for leveraging your book, you can ensure that it continues to generate value and support your business objectives for years to come.

Integrating your book into your overall business strategy requires careful planning and execution, but the payoff can be significant. By aligning your book with your broader goals, incorporating it into your existing offerings, and leveraging it as a long-term asset, you can create a powerful tool that drives business growth, establishes your thought leadership, and sets you apart in a crowded market.

Remember, your book is not just a one-time project, but a valuable resource that can support and enhance every aspect of your business. By taking a strategic and integrated approach to your book, you can maximize its impact and achieve the long-term success you deserve.

Setting Milestones and Staying Accountable

Writing and promoting a book is a significant undertaking that requires dedication, focus, and accountability. To ensure that you stay on track and make steady progress towards your goals, it's essential to set clear milestones and implement systems that keep you motivated and accountable.

To begin, establish a set of clear, achievable milestones that break down your book-writing and promotion journey into manageable steps. These milestones should be specific, measurable, and time-bound, allowing you to track your progress and celebrate your accomplishments along the way. For example, your milestones might include:

1. Completing your book outline and chapter summaries by a specific date
2. Writing a certain number of words or pages each week or month
3. Completing your first draft by a target deadline
4. Securing a certain number of pre-orders or reviews before your book launch
5. Booking a specific number of speaking engagements or media appearances within the first six months of your book's release

By setting these milestones upfront, you create a roadmap for your book-writing and promotion journey, making it easier to stay focused and motivated even when challenges arise.

To support your progress and keep yourself accountable, it's important to implement systems and support mechanisms that help you stay on track. This may involve:

1. Creating a detailed project plan or timeline that outlines the specific tasks and deadlines associated with each milestone
2. Breaking down larger tasks into smaller, more manageable steps that you can tackle on a daily or weekly basis
3. Enlisting the support of an accountability partner, writing group, or coach who can provide guidance, feedback, and encouragement along the way
4. Using productivity tools or apps, such as time-tracking software or project management platforms, to help you stay organized and efficient
5. Establishing a regular writing routine or schedule that allows you to make consistent progress, even when life gets busy

By implementing these systems and support mechanisms, you create a structure that helps you stay focused, motivated, and accountable, even when the going gets tough.

As you work towards your milestones, it's important to regularly assess your progress and make adjustments as needed. This may involve:

1. Setting aside time each week or month to review your project plan and evaluate your progress against your milestones
2. Identifying any obstacles or challenges that are holding you back and brainstorming strategies to overcome them
3. Celebrating your successes and accomplishments along the way, using them as motivation to keep pushing forward
4. Adjusting your milestones or timeline as needed to account for unexpected delays or changes in your circumstances
5. Seeking out additional support or resources if you find yourself struggling to make progress or stay on track

By regularly assessing your progress and making adjustments as required, you can ensure that you remain flexible and adaptable, even as your book-writing and promotion journey evolves.

Remember, writing and promoting a book is a marathon, not a sprint. By setting clear milestones, implementing supportive systems, and regularly assessing your progress, you can maintain the focus, motivation, and accountability you need to see your project through to completion.

Embrace the journey, celebrate your successes along the way, and trust that with dedication and perseverance, you will achieve your goal of creating a powerful, impactful book that transforms your business and your life.

Celebrating Your Book's Launch and Impact

The day has finally arrived—your book is launched and ready to make its mark on the world. This is a moment to celebrate, not just the culmination of your hard work and dedication, but also the beginning of a new chapter in your business and your life.

To mark this milestone, consider planning a memorable and impactful book launch event or campaign. This could be a virtual or in-person gathering that brings together your team, supporters, and readers to celebrate your achievement and generate buzz around your book. Some ideas for your launch event might include:

1. A live reading or Q&A session where you share excerpts from your book and engage with your audience
2. A panel discussion featuring experts or influencers in your field who can speak to the importance and relevance of your book's themes
3. A social media campaign or challenge that encourages readers to share their own experiences and insights related to your book
4. A contest or giveaway that rewards early adopters and generates excitement around your book's release

Whatever format you choose, your launch event should be designed to create a sense of excitement, community, and momentum around your book, setting the stage for its success in the weeks and months to come.

As you celebrate your book's launch, be sure to take a moment to acknowledge and appreciate the team and supporters who have contributed to your success along the way. This may include:

1. Your ghostwriter, editor, and other publishing professionals who helped bring your book to life
2. Your family, friends, and colleagues who provided moral support and encouragement throughout the writing and promotion process
3. Your early readers, reviewers, and endorsers who helped validate your book's value and spread the word to their networks
4. Your clients, customers, and followers who have supported your work and believed in your vision

Take the time to express your gratitude and appreciation for these individuals, whether through personal notes, public acknowledgments, or special gestures of thanks. Recognizing the role that others have played in your success not only strengthens your relationships but also sets a tone of generosity and collaboration that will serve you well in the future.

Finally, as you bask in the glow of your book's launch, take a moment to reflect on the journey that brought you to this point. Consider the challenges you overcame, the lessons you learned, and the growth you experienced along the way. Reflect on the impact that your book has already had—on your own thinking, on your business, and on the lives of your readers.

Use this reflection as an opportunity to set intentions and goals for the future. How will you continue to leverage your book's success to drive your business forward? What new opportunities or partnerships might your book open up? How will you continue to engage and support your readers in the months and years to come?

By taking the time to celebrate your book's launch, acknowledge your supporters, and reflect on your journey, you not only honor the significant achievement of bringing your book to life but also set the stage for continued growth and success. Remember, your book's launch is not the end of your journey, but rather the beginning of a new and exciting chapter in your business and your life.

Embrace the possibilities, stay open to new opportunities, and continue to lead with the same passion, dedication, and vision that brought you to this point. Your book is a powerful tool for transformation—not just for your readers, but for yourself and your business as well. Celebrate your success, and look forward to the many exciting chapters yet to come.

Chapter 9

Bringing Your Book to Life with Our Ghostwriting Services

For many entrepreneurs, consultants, and business leaders, the idea of writing a book can seem like an insurmountable challenge. Despite recognizing the potential benefits of authoring a book, the reality of the writing process often presents significant obstacles that can derail even the most well-intentioned professionals.

One of the most common challenges faced by busy professionals is the lack of time. Running a successful business demands constant attention, leaving little room for the focused, uninterrupted writing sessions necessary to create a high-quality book. Between client meetings, strategic planning, and day-to-day operations, finding dedicated time to write can feel like an impossible task.

Many professionals struggle with the actual writing process itself. While they may be experts in their field, translating that knowledge into a well-structured, engaging book requires a different skill set. Lack of writing experience or confidence can lead to frustration, writer's block, and a sense of inadequacy that can quickly extinguish the initial enthusiasm for the project.

Even for those who possess strong writing skills, organizing complex ideas and structuring a cohesive narrative can be a daunting task. Business professionals often have a wealth of knowledge and insights to share, but determining how to effectively convey that information in a logical, reader-friendly manner can be overwhelming.

These challenges frequently lead to abandoned book projects, unrealized potential, and a sense of missed opportunity. However, it's important to recognize that these obstacles are not insurmountable. By partnering with experienced ghostwriters who specialize in helping business professionals bring their books to life, you can overcome these challenges and unlock the transformative power of authoring a book.

In the following sections, we'll explore how our ghostwriting services can help you navigate the challenges of writing a book as a busy professional. From providing the time-saving support and expertise you need, to ensuring your book captures your unique voice and message, our team is dedicated to helping you achieve your book-writing goals and leverage your book for business growth.

How Our Ghostwriting Services Can Help

Recognizing the challenges that busy professionals face when writing a book, our ghostwriting services are designed to provide the support, expertise, and guidance you need to bring your book to life. By partnering with our experienced, professional writers, you can overcome the obstacles that often derail book projects and ensure that your book is of the highest quality, aligning with your vision and goals.

Our team of ghostwriters consists of seasoned professionals who have a proven track record of collaborating with business leaders, entrepreneurs, and consultants to create compelling, authoritative books. With their extensive writing experience and deep understanding of the book-writing process, our ghostwriters can help you navigate the complexities of crafting a well-structured, engaging book that captures your unique voice and message.

When you work with our ghostwriting services, you gain access to a dedicated writing partner who will be with you every step of the way. From the initial planning stages to the final manuscript, your ghostwriter will provide the guidance, support, and accountability you need to stay on track and make steady progress toward your book-writing goals.

Your ghostwriter will take the time to understand your vision, target audience, and desired outcomes for your book. They will work closely with you to extract your knowledge, insights, and experiences, and transform them into a cohesive, compelling narrative that resonates with your readers. By asking the right questions, providing thoughtful feedback, and offering expert advice, your ghostwriter will ensure that your book effectively communicates your message and achieves your desired impact.

Throughout the writing process, your ghostwriter will serve as a sounding board, helping you refine your ideas, clarify your thoughts, and overcome any creative blocks or challenges that arise. They will provide regular updates, revisions, and opportunities for feedback, ensuring that you remain fully engaged and satisfied with the direction and progress of your book.

In addition to the hands-on writing support, our ghostwriting services also offer project management and quality control expertise. Your ghostwriter will help you establish a clear timeline, set milestones, and keep your book project on track. They will also manage the editing, proofreading, and formatting processes, ensuring that your final manuscript meets the highest standards of quality and professionalism.

By leveraging our ghostwriting services, you can have confidence that your book will be well-written, carefully structured, and aligned with your vision. Our ghostwriters are committed to delivering a final product that exceeds your expectations and positions you as an authoritative voice in your industry.

Our Ghostwriting Process

At the heart of our ghostwriting services lies a well-defined, collaborative process designed to ensure the successful creation of your book. Our approach is built on a foundation of open communication, trust, and a shared commitment to bringing your vision to life. Let's take a closer look at the key stages of our ghostwriting process.

Discovery: Understanding Your Needs, Goals, and Approach The first step in our ghostwriting process is a comprehensive discovery phase. During this stage, your ghostwriter will take the time to deeply understand your goals, target audience, and desired outcomes for your book. Through a series of in-depth conversations and questionnaires, we will explore your unique perspective, experiences, and the key messages you want to convey through your book.

Our discovery process goes beyond surface-level details. We delve into your motivations for writing the book, the impact you hope to achieve, and the specific ways in which you envision your book supporting your business growth. By gaining a thorough understanding of your needs and objectives, we lay the foundation for a successful collaboration and ensure that your book aligns with your overall strategy.

Developing a detailed outline and content plan, with a clear understanding of your goals and vision, your ghostwriter will work closely with you to develop a detailed outline and content plan for your book. This crucial step helps to organize your ideas, structure your narrative, and ensure that your book flows logically from one chapter to the next.

Your ghostwriter will collaborate with you to identify the key themes, topics, and subtopics that will form the backbone of your book. They will help you determine the most effective way to present your information, whether through storytelling, case studies, practical examples, or a combination of techniques. The outline serves as a roadmap for the writing process, ensuring that your book remains focused, engaging, and aligned with your objectives.

In addition to the outline, your ghostwriter will create a content plan that breaks down the writing process into manageable stages. This plan will include milestones, deadlines, and regular check-ins to keep your book project on track and ensure a smooth, efficient collaboration.

Roughing, Writing, and Revising With the outline and content plan in place, your ghostwriter will begin the hands-on writing process. This stage typically involves a rotation of "roughing" (a draft), writing, and revising to ensure that your book meets the highest standards of quality and effectively conveys your message.

We will start by roughing out the content for each chapter, creating a basic structure and flow for the information. This rough draft serves as a starting point for the more detailed writing process, al lowing your ghostwriter to refine the language, develop your unique voice, and ensure that each chapter builds upon the previous ones.

As the writing progresses, your ghostwriter will share regular updates and drafts with you for review and feedback. This collaborative approach ensures that you remain fully engaged in the process and that the book remains true to your vision. Your ghostwriter will incorporate your insights, make necessary revisions, and work with you to refine the manuscript until it meets your expectations.

Throughout the writing and revising stages, your ghostwriter will pay close attention to the overall structure, pacing, and coherence of your book. They will ensure that your ideas are presented in a logical, compelling manner and that your book delivers value to your target audience. By the end of this stage, you will have a polished, professional manuscript that is ready for the next steps in the publishing process.

Our ghostwriting process is designed to provide you with the support, expertise, and peace of mind you need to create a high-quality book that achieves your goals. By partnering with our experienced ghostwriters and following our proven approach, you can transform your ideas and insights into a powerful tool for business growth and thought leadership.

The Benefits of Working with Our Team

Collaborating with our professional ghostwriting team offers numerous advantages for busy business leaders, entrepreneurs, and consultants who want to create a high-impact book while maximizing their time and energy. By leveraging our expertise and support, you can enjoy a seamless, rewarding book-writing experience that results in a powerful tool for your business growth. Let's explore some key benefits of working with our ghostwriters.

Saving Time and Energy While Still Creating a High-Impact Book One of the most significant advantages of partnering with our ghostwriters is the ability to save valuable time and energy throughout the book-writing process. As a busy professional, your time is a precious commodity, and dedicating countless hours to writing and refining a book can be a daunting prospect. By entrusting your book project to our experienced ghostwriters, you can focus on running your business and serving your clients while still achieving your goal of creating a high-impact book.

Our team will handle the heavy lifting of the writing process, from research and outlining to drafting and revising. They will work efficiently and effectively to transform your ideas and insights into a well-crafted, polished manuscript, allowing you to allocate your time and energy to the areas where you can make the greatest impact.

Leveraging Our Expertise in Book Structure, Storytelling, and Publishing When you collaborate with our ghostwriters, you gain access to a wealth of knowledge and expertise in the areas of book structure, storytelling, and publishing. Our team consists of seasoned professionals who have a deep understanding of what makes a book engaging, compelling, and effective in today's marketplace.

Your ghostwriting team will work closely with you to develop a strong, logical structure for your book, ensuring that your ideas are presented in a clear and impactful manner. They will help you identify the most powerful stories, examples, and case studies to illustrate your points and keep your readers engaged from start to finish.

We stay up-to-date with the latest trends and best practices in the publishing industry. We can provide valuable insights and guidance on topics such as book design, formatting, and distribution, helping you make informed decisions that maximize your book's visibility and reach.

Receiving Objective, Professional Feedback and Guidance Another significant benefit of working with our ghostwriters is the opportunity to receive objective, professional feedback and guidance throughout the book-writing process. As an expert in your field, it can be challenging to step back and assess your own ideas and writing with a critical eye. Our ghostwriters provide an unbiased, external perspective that can help you refine your message, clarify your thoughts, and communicate your insights more effectively.

Your team will offer constructive feedback and suggestions based on their professional experience and understanding of your target audience. They will help you identify areas where your book can be strengthened, provide guidance on how to overcome any challenges or roadblocks, and offer ongoing support and encouragement to keep you motivated and on track.

Ensuring Your Book Captures Your Unique Voice, Knowledge, and Experiences One of the most important aspects of a successful book is its ability to authentically capture the author's unique voice, knowledge, and experiences. Our ghostwriters are skilled at collaborating closely with clients to ensure that their book truly reflects their personality, expertise, and perspective.

Through in-depth interviews, discussions, and reviews of your existing materials, your ghostwriter will gain a thorough understanding of your style, tone, and messaging preferences. They will work diligently to infuse your book with your distinct voice, ensuring that it resonates with your target audience and accurately represents your brand and vision.

By capturing your unique insights, stories, and experiences, your ghostwriter will help you create a book that sets you apart as an authority in your field and provides genuine value to your readers.

Collaborating with your team offers a wide range of benefits that can help you create a high-impact book while optimizing your time, energy, and resources. From leveraging our expertise in book structure and storytelling to receiving objective feedback and ensuring your unique voice shines through, our ghostwriters are committed to helping you achieve your book-writing goals and unlock the power of your ideas.

AI-Assisted Ghostwriting: Enhancing the Writing Process

As technology continues to advance, our ghostwriting services have embraced the power of artificial intelligence (AI) to enhance the writing process and deliver even better results for our clients. By incorporating AI tools into our workflow, we can streamline research, generate valuable content ideas, and ultimately create higher-quality books in less time. However, it's essential to understand the role of AI in our process and how our human writers ensure the authenticity and quality of every project.

How We Utilize AI Tools to Streamline Research and Content Generation Our ghostwriting team leverages state-of-the-art AI tools to assist with various aspects of the book-writing process. One key area where AI shines is in the realm of research. By utilizing AI-powered search engines and data analysis tools, we can quickly gather relevant information, statistics, and case studies related to your book's topic. This allows our ghostwriters to build a comprehensive knowledge base and identify unique insights that can strengthen your book's content.

In addition to research, AI can also play a valuable role in content generation. Advanced language models and writing assistants can help our ghostwriters brainstorm ideas, outline chapters, and even draft initial content based on your input and preferences. These AI-generated snippets serve as a starting point, providing our writers with a foundation to build upon and refine.

The Role of Human Writers in Overseeing and Refining AI-Generated Content While AI tools can significantly enhance the writing process, it's crucial to understand that they are not a replacement for human expertise and creativity. Our experienced ghostwriters play a vital role in overseeing and refining any AI-generated content to ensure that it meets our high standards of quality and aligns with your unique voice and vision.

Our ghostwriters (your team) will carefully review and edit AI-generated text, checking for accuracy, coherence, and adherence to your desired tone and style. They use their deep understanding of your industry, target audience, and objectives to shape the content, adding context, nuance, and personal anecdotes that resonate with your readers.

Human writers are essential for weaving together the various elements of your book—from the AI-generated snippets to the insights gleaned from your interviews and existing materials—into a cohesive, compelling narrative. They ensure that your book flows logically, maintains a consistent voice, and delivers value to your target audience.

Our Commitment to Maintaining Authenticity and Quality in Every Project At our core, we are committed to maintaining the highest levels of authenticity and quality in every book project we undertake. While AI tools can assist in the writing process, we firmly believe that the human touch is essential for creating a book that truly captures your unique perspective and expertise.

We work closely with you throughout the writing process, ensuring that your book remains true to your vision and authentically represents your ideas and experiences. They take the time to understand your goals, preferences, and communication style, and they collaborate with you to refine the content until it meets your expectations.

We also have rigorous quality control measures in place to ensure that every book we produce meets our exacting standards. Our editing and proofreading process involves multiple rounds of review by our team of experienced professionals, guaranteeing that your final manuscript is polished, error-free, and ready for publication.

Addressing Common Concerns and Misconceptions about AI in Writing We understand that some clients may have concerns or misconceptions about the use of AI in the writing process. It's important to address these issues head-on and provide clarity about the role of AI in our ghostwriting services.

One common concern is that AI-generated content may lack the depth, nuance, and personal touch that readers expect from a book. However, as we've emphasized, our human ghostwriters are integral to the process, ensuring that your book captures your unique voice and perspective. AI tools serve as a complement to our writers' skills and expertise, not a replacement.

Another misconception is that AI can write an entire book independently. While AI has made significant strides in recent years, it is not yet capable of autonomously creating a coherent, high-quality, long-form book. Human oversight, direction, and refinement are essential for a successful book project.

At this point, AI can't write long-form content by itself. Humans must coordinate the entire project, from planning and research to writing and editing. To effectively leverage AI in the writing process, you need people who deeply understand the specific type of writing being done, whether it's nonfiction, adventure, romance, or any other genre. You also need people who know how machines think—and can speak their language, both literally and figuratively. Our ghostwriters possess this unique combination of skills, allowing them to harness the power of AI while maintaining the human touch that makes your book truly special.

By combining the efficiency and insight of AI tools with the creativity and expertise of our human ghostwriters, we can deliver a superior book-writing experience for our clients. Our AI-assisted approach allows us to create high-quality books more efficiently, without compromising on authenticity or personal connection. With our ghostwriting services, you can be confident that your book will be a powerful, engaging, and authentic representation of your ideas and expertise.

Samples and Privacy

When it comes to ghostwriting, discretion and confidentiality are paramount. Our clients trust us to help them share their ideas, experiences, and expertise with the world, and we take that responsibility seriously. As such, we adhere to strict privacy protocols and do not publicize or share information about our prior work without explicit permission from our clients.

The "Ghost" in Ghostwriting: Protecting Our Clients' Confidentiality The very nature of ghostwriting is rooted in anonymity. When you work with a ghostwriter, you are entrusting them to capture your voice, knowledge, and unique perspective, but ultimately, the book is yours. The ghostwriter remains in the background, allowing you to claim full authorship and ownership of the work.

To maintain this confidentiality, we do not publicly showcase or advertise the books we have written for our clients. We respect their privacy, and their right to decide whether to disclose their use of a ghostwriter. This commitment to discretion is a fundamental aspect of our ghostwriting services, and it is something we take very seriously.

Extensive Sample Work: Demonstrating Our Expertise and Capabilities While we cannot share the specific books we have written for our clients, we understand the importance of providing prospective clients with a clear sense of our writing skills, style, and expertise. That's why we have developed an extensive collection of sample work that showcases our capabilities across a wide range of topics and genres.

Our sample work is designed to give you a comprehensive understanding of the quality, depth, and versatility of our writing. From engaging introductions to thought-provoking chapters, our samples demonstrate our ability to craft compelling, well-structured content that resonates with readers.

By reviewing our sample work, you can gain confidence in our ghostwriters' skills and expertise. You'll see firsthand how we can capture different voices, styles, and tones, and how we can effectively communicate complex ideas in a clear, accessible manner. Our samples serve as a testament to the high standards we maintain in every project we undertake.

Our Unique Approach: Building Trust and Confidence Before Commitment We recognize that entrusting your book project to a ghostwriter is a significant decision, and we want to ensure that you feel fully confident and comfortable before moving forward. That's why we have developed a unique approach to our ghostwriting services that sets us apart from others in the industry.

Unlike many ghostwriting companies that require upfront payment or commitment, we do not charge a single penny, nor do we ask you to agree to work with us, until after the entire discovery and planning process is completed. This means that you have the opportunity to experience our expertise, professionalism, and dedication firsthand, without any financial risk or obligation.

During the discovery and planning phase, our ghostwriters will work closely with you to understand your goals, target audience, and desired outcome for your book. We'll collaborate with you to develop a detailed outline, content plan, and writing strategy that aligns with your vision. Throughout this process, you'll have the chance to assess our skills, communication style, and ability to capture your unique voice and perspective.

Only after this comprehensive discovery and planning process is complete will we discuss the next steps and potential collaboration. By this point, you'll have a clear understanding of our capabilities, a well-defined roadmap for your book, and the confidence to make an informed decision about moving forward with our ghostwriting services.

This unique approach not only demonstrates our commitment to transparency and client satisfaction but also allows us to build a strong foundation of trust and understanding with each client. By investing time and effort upfront, without any financial commitment from you, we can ensure that we are the right fit for your project and that we can deliver a book that exceeds your expectations.

Our combination of strict privacy protocols, extensive sample work, and a client-centric approach to discovery and planning sets us apart as a ghostwriting service provider. We are dedicated to providing you with the highest level of confidentiality, expertise, and support throughout your book-writing journey, and we are confident that our unique approach will give you the peace of mind and assurance you need to bring your book to life.

Is Our Ghostwriting Service Right for You?

Choosing the right ghostwriting service is a crucial decision that can significantly impact the success of your book project. While we are confident in our ability to deliver high-quality, impactful books for our clients, we also recognize that our services may not be the perfect fit for everyone. In this section, we'll help you assess whether our ghostwriting service aligns with your needs and goals, and provide guidance on alternative options if we're not the best match.

Our Specialization: Expert Books and Long-Form Executive Branding At our core, we specialize in crafting expert books and other forms of long-form content for executive branding. Our ghostwriters excel at working with business leaders, entrepreneurs, consultants, and other professionals who want to share their knowledge, insights, and experiences to establish themselves as thought leaders in their industries.

If your goal is to create a book that showcases your expertise, solidifies your authority, and helps you stand out in your field, then our ghostwriting service is an excellent fit for you. We have a proven track record of helping clients transform their ideas and experiences into compelling, well-structured books that resonate with their target audiences.

What We Don't Do: Memoirs and Fiction While we are passionate about helping our clients share their knowledge and expertise, there are certain types of books that fall outside our area of specialization. Specifically, we do not offer ghostwriting services for memoirs or fictional works.

Memoirs, which are deeply personal accounts of an individual's life experiences, require a unique approach to capturing the author's voice, emotions, and memories. While AI technology has made significant strides in recent years, we believe that crafting a truly authentic and compelling memoir is not yet possible with AI-assisted writing. The nuances, complexities, and emotional depth required for a powerful memoir are still best achieved through close collaboration between the author and a skilled human ghostwriter.

Similarly, although there have been some interesting developments in AI-assisted fiction writing, it is not a core focus of our ghostwriting service. Writing compelling, engaging fictional stories requires a different set of skills and techniques than those employed in our expert book writing process. As such, we have chosen to concentrate our efforts on our area of expertise, ensuring that we can deliver the highest quality results for our clients.

Assessing Your Book-Writing Needs and Goals To determine whether our ghostwriting service is the right fit for you, it's essential to take a close look at your book-writing needs and goals. Consider questions such as:

- What is the primary purpose of your book? Is it to share your expertise, establish your authority, or promote your brand?
- Who is your target audience? Are you aiming to reach professionals in your industry, potential clients, or a broader general audience?
- What type of content do you envision for your book? Will it be focused on practical advice, strategic insights, or thought-provoking ideas?
- How do you plan to use your book as part of your overall business or personal branding strategy?

If your answers align with our specialization in expert books and long-form executive branding content, then our ghostwriting service may be an excellent choice for bringing your book to life.

Alternative Options to Consider If, after assessing your needs and goals, you determine that our ghostwriting service isn't the best fit for your project, there are several alternative options to consider:

1. Memoir ghostwriting services: If you're looking to write a personal memoir, seek out ghostwriters or agencies that specialize in this genre. They will have the necessary skills and experience to help you capture your unique voice and tell your story in a compelling way.
2. Fiction writing coaches or editors: For those interested in writing a novel or short story collection, working with a fiction writing coach or editor can provide the guidance and support you need to bring your creative vision to life. These professionals can help you refine your plot, characters, and writing style.
3. DIY book writing: If you have the time, skills, and motivation to write your book yourself, there are numerous resources available to help you through the process. From writing

courses and workshops to online communities and self-publishing platforms, you can find the tools and support you need to bring your book to fruition.

4. Traditional ghostwriting services: For those who prefer a more traditional, human-centric approach to ghostwriting, there are many skilled ghostwriters who do not incorporate AI into their writing process. These professionals rely on their own writing expertise and close collaboration with clients to craft high-quality books.

Do We Write Without AI? One question we often encounter is whether we offer ghostwriting services without the use of AI. The short answer is no. As mentioned earlier, we firmly believe that the judicious use of AI technology, combined with the skills and oversight of our human ghostwriters, allows us to deliver exceptional results for our clients.

We understand that the idea of AI-assisted writing may seem daunting or even impossible to some. However, our extensive portfolio of successful projects and satisfied clients is a testament to the effectiveness of our approach. By leveraging the power of AI, we can streamline the research and writing process, generate valuable insights and content ideas, and ultimately create books of the highest caliber.

It's important to note that AI is not a replacement for human expertise and creativity but rather a powerful tool that enhances our ghostwriters' abilities. Our team consists of skilled writers and editors who deeply understand the intricacies of crafting expert books and long-form content. They know how to work with AI technology, harnessing its capabilities while maintaining the human touch that is essential for creating authentic, engaging, and impactful books.

In today's rapidly evolving digital landscape, we believe that embracing AI-assisted writing is not just a choice but a necessity for staying at the forefront of the ghostwriting industry. By combining the best of human expertise and artificial intelligence, we can deliver unparalleled value to our clients and help them achieve their book-writing goals more efficiently and effectively than ever before.

Ultimately, the decision to work with our AI-assisted ghostwriting service is a personal one that depends on your unique needs, preferences, and comfort level with technology. We encourage you to review our sample work, ask questions, and discuss your project with our team to determine whether we are the right fit for you. If not, we are happy to provide guidance and recommendations on alternative options that may better suit your needs.

Taking the Next Step

If you've made it this far, you're probably excited about the possibility of bringing your book idea to life and harnessing the power of a well-crafted book to elevate your business or personal brand. Whether you're confident that our AI-assisted ghostwriting service is the right fit for you, or still have questions and concerns, we encourage you to take the next step and reach out to our team for a more in-depth discussion about your project.

Complimentary Discovery and Planning Process We understand that committing to a ghostwriting service is a significant decision, and we want to ensure that you have all the information you need to make an informed choice. That's why we offer a complimentary discovery and planning process, where you can explore the potential of your book idea with our team of experts, without any cost or obligation.

During this discovery phase, we'll dive deep into your goals, target audience, and unique perspective, helping you refine your book concept and develop a clear vision for your project. Our ghostwriters will work with you to create a detailed outline and table of contents, giving you a comprehensive overview of your book's structure and content.

This process serves several key purposes:

1. It allows you to experience our team's expertise and approach firsthand, giving you a better understanding of how we work and what you can expect from our ghostwriting service.
2. It provides you with a tangible roadmap for your book, helping you visualize the final product and its potential impact on your business or personal brand.
3. It gives our team the opportunity to offer personalized recommendations and strategies for making your book as impactful and successful as possible.

By the end of the discovery and planning process, you'll have a clear sense of your book's direction, a detailed outline to guide the writing process, and the insights you need to make an informed decision about moving forward with our ghostwriting service.

No Cost, No Obligation We believe in the value of our AI-assisted ghostwriting approach, and we're confident that once you experience our expertise and dedication firsthand, you'll be excited to continue working with us. However, we also recognize that this initial discovery and planning process is a valuable service in its own right, and we're happy to offer it to you at no cost and with no obligation to continue working with us.

If, after completing the discovery and planning process, you decide that our ghostwriting service isn't the right fit for you, you're free to walk away with no further commitment. You'll still have gained valuable insights into your book idea, a clearer sense of direction, and a detailed outline that you can use to guide your writing process, whether you choose to work with another ghostwriter or tackle the project on your own.

We believe that this risk-free approach is the best way to help potential clients make informed decisions and ensure that we're the right fit for their needs. It's just one more way that we prioritize our clients' success and satisfaction above all else.

Take the First Step Today If you're ready to explore the potential of your book idea and take the first step toward bringing your vision to life, we invite you to contact our team today. You will find all our contact information on the website, GhostwriterMarketing.com.

When you reach out, one of our friendly and knowledgeable team members will be happy to answer any questions you may have, provide additional information about our services, and schedule your complimentary discovery and planning session.

Don't let your book idea remain just an idea any longer. Take action today and discover the power of our AI-assisted ghostwriting service to help you share your expertise, establish your authority, and achieve your business or personal branding goals. We look forward to hearing from you and helping you bring your book to life!

Unleashing the Power of Your Book

As we come to the end of our journey together, let's take a moment to reflect on the key lessons and insights we've covered throughout this book. *Take the Book by the Horns: Grow your business—as a published expert!* has been a comprehensive guide to understanding the transformative power of a book and how it can be leveraged to skyrocket your business success.

We began by exploring the changing landscape of business and expertise, and how traditional marketing and sales strategies are losing their effectiveness in today's competitive market. We then delved into the unique benefits of a book compared to other content formats, showcasing real-world examples of businesses that have achieved remarkable growth and success through their books.

Throughout the book, we've emphasized the importance of positioning yourself as an expert and authority in your field. By sharing your unique perspective, experiences, and insights through your book, you can establish unshakable credibility and attract higher-quality clients who are eager to work with you.

We've also explored the practical strategies and techniques for leveraging your book to achieve specific business objectives. From using your book as a powerful lead generation tool and conversation starter to integrating it into your sales process and leveraging it for speaking engagements and media opportunities, we've covered a wide range of tactics for maximizing the impact of your book.

One of the key themes throughout this book has been the power of storytelling, and the importance of crafting a compelling narrative that resonates with your target audience. We've discussed techniques for weaving engaging stories and anecdotes into your book, balancing storytelling with practical advice, and creating a strong emotional connection with your readers.

We've also tackled the unique challenges of writing a book as a business professional, from time constraints and lack of writing experience to the difficulty of organizing complex ideas and structuring content. By exploring the power of ghostwriting and the benefits of working with a professional writer, we've shown how even the busiest entrepreneurs and executives can bring their book ideas to life.

Finally, we've provided a comprehensive action plan for leveraging your book for business growth. From developing your book content strategy and choosing the right publishing path to crafting your promotion and distribution plan and integrating your book into your overall business strategy, we've offered step-by-step guidance for ensuring the success of your book project.

As you reflect on your key takeaways and "aha" moments from this book, we encourage you to embrace the transformative potential of writing a book for your business. Whether you're looking to establish your authority, attract higher-quality clients, or open doors to new opportunities, your book can be the ultimate tool for achieving your goals.

Remember, writing a book is not just about sharing your knowledge and expertise; it's about leaving a lasting legacy and making a profound impact on your industry and the lives of your readers. By putting the strategies and insights from this book into action, you can unleash the power of your book and take your business to new heights.

So, what are you waiting for? It's time to start your book-writing journey and transform your business through the power of your words. The world is waiting for your message, and your success story is just waiting to be written. Let's make it happen together.

Overcoming Obstacles and Embracing the Journey

As you embark on your book-writing journey, it's natural to encounter fears, doubts, and challenges along the way. Writing a book is a significant undertaking, and it's common to feel overwhelmed or uncertain at times. However, it's essential to remember that these obstacles are not insurmountable, and that every challenge you face is an opportunity for growth and development.

One of the most common fears among aspiring authors is the fear of not being "good enough" or not having anything valuable to say. You may question your expertise, your writing abilities, or the uniqueness of your message. These doubts can be paralyzing, causing you to procrastinate or even abandon your book project altogether.

But here's the truth: your perspective is unique, and your experiences and insights have the power to make a real difference in the lives of your readers. Your book doesn't have to be perfect; it just has to be authentic and valuable. By sharing your knowledge and expertise with honesty and vulnerability, you can connect with your audience on a deep level and establish yourself as a trusted authority in your field.

Another common challenge in the book-writing process is finding the time and discipline to write consistently. As a busy professional, you likely have a multitude of competing priorities and demands on your time. It can be easy to let your book project fall by the wayside when you're juggling client work, business operations, and personal responsibilities.

The key to overcoming this challenge is to treat your book as a priority and to develop a writing routine that works for you. Whether it's setting aside dedicated writing time each day, using time-blocking techniques to manage your schedule, or enlisting the support of a writing coach or accountability partner, there are many strategies you can use to stay on track and make consistent progress on your book.

It's also important to reframe the book-writing journey as an opportunity for personal and professional growth. Writing a book is not just about the end product; it's about the process of clarifying your ideas, refining your message, and developing your voice as a thought leader. Every step of the journey, from the initial ideation to the final editing and promotion, is a chance to learn, grow, and stretch yourself in new ways.

Embrace the challenges and obstacles as opportunities to build resilience, develop new skills, and deepen your self-awareness. When you approach the book-writing process with a growth mindset, you open yourself up to a world of possibility and transformation.

Finally, remember that you don't have to go it alone. Surround yourself with a support system of mentors, colleagues, and loved ones who believe in your vision and are cheering you on every step of the way. Seek out communities of fellow authors and thought leaders who can offer guidance, encouragement, and accountability. And don't be afraid to ask for help when you need it, whether it's hiring a ghostwriter to help you bring your ideas to life or enlisting the support of a book coach to keep you on track and motivated.

Writing a book is a journey of self-discovery, personal growth, and professional transformation. By embracing the challenges and obstacles as opportunities for development, and by staying committed to your vision and your message, you can unleash the power of your book and create a lasting impact on your business and the world around you.

So, take a deep breath, trust in the process, and remember that every step of the journey is bringing you closer to your goal. You have a message worth sharing, and the world is waiting to hear it. Keep writing, keep growing, and keep believing in the transformative power of your words.

Envisioning Your Book's Impact and Legacy

As you near the end of your book-writing journey, it's important to take a step back and envision the long-term impact and legacy of your work. Your book has the power to transform not only your own business and life but also the lives of your readers and the broader industry you serve.

Take a moment to visualize the ripple effect of your book's message and insights. Imagine your ideal reader, perhaps a fellow entrepreneur or professional, picking up your book and experiencing a profound shift in their mindset and approach to their work. Picture them implementing the strategies and techniques you've shared, and seeing tangible results in their business growth and success.

Now, multiply that impact by the number of readers your book has the potential to reach. Each person who engages with your book has the opportunity to take your ideas and insights and apply them in their own unique way, creating a cascade of positive change and transformation.

But the impact of your book doesn't stop there. By establishing yourself as an authority and thought leader in your field, you have the power to shape the conversation and direction of your industry as a whole. Your book can serve as a catalyst for new ideas, innovations, and best practices that elevate the standard of excellence in your field.

Imagine your book being cited in industry publications, discussed at conferences and events, and used as a resource in training and education programs. Your insights and perspectives could become the foundation for a new paradigm of thinking and operating, influencing the way businesses approach challenges and opportunities for years to come.

Beyond the immediate benefits of business growth and increased visibility, your book has the potential to leave a lasting legacy that extends far beyond your own career and lifetime. By sharing your unique story, expertise, and vision, you have the opportunity to make a meaningful and enduring contribution to your field and the world at large.

Imagine your book being passed down to future generations of entrepreneurs and professionals, continuing to inspire and guide them long after you're gone. Your words and ideas could become a timeless source of wisdom and inspiration, leaving a legacy of impact and transformation that touches countless lives.

As you contemplate the broader significance of your work, it's natural to feel a sense of responsibility and purpose. Your book is not just a business tool, or a personal accomplishment; it's a gift to the world, a way of sharing your unique perspective and making a difference in the lives of others.

Embrace this sense of purpose and let it fuel your motivation and commitment to bringing your book to life. When you approach your book-writing journey with a clear vision of the impact and legacy you want to create, you tap into a deeper source of inspiration and drive.

Remember, your book has the power to change lives, transform businesses, and shape the future of your industry. By pouring your heart, expertise, and vision into your work, you have the opportunity to create something truly extraordinary and enduring.

So, as you move forward on your book-writing journey, keep this vision of impact and legacy at the forefront of your mind. Let it guide your choices, inform your content, and inspire you to create a book that truly matters.

Your words have power, and your message has the potential to resonate far beyond the pages of your book. Embrace the opportunity to make a lasting difference, and trust in the ripple effect of your work. Your book is not just a reflection of who you are; it's a testament to the impact you're meant to have on the world.

Throughout this book, we've explored the transformative power of writing a book and how it can be the ultimate tool for business growth and personal impact. You've learned the strategies, techniques, and mindset shifts necessary to leverage your book for increased visibility, authority, and success.

Now, it's time to take action and turn your book idea into a reality. The world needs your message, and your unique perspective has the power to make a profound difference in the lives of your readers and the future of your industry.

If you're ready to embark on your book-writing journey, here's a clear and actionable roadmap to get you started:

1. Define your book's purpose and unique value proposition. Clarity is key when it comes to writing a book that resonates with your target audience. Take time to reflect on the specific outcomes you want to achieve with your book, the transformation you want to create for your readers, and the unique insights and experiences you bring to the table.
2. Identify your ideal reader and target audience. Understanding who you're writing for is essential to crafting a message that truly connects and provides value. Create a detailed profile of your ideal reader, including their challenges, goals, and preferences, and use this as a guide for your book's content and style.
3. Develop a comprehensive outline and content plan. A well-structured book is the foundation of a compelling and impactful message. Take time to map out your book's key

themes, chapters, and ideas, ensuring a logical flow and progression that keeps your readers engaged from start to finish.

4. Consider partnering with a skilled ghostwriter to bring your book to life. Writing a book is a significant undertaking, and collaborating with a professional ghostwriter can help you save time, energy, and ensure a high-quality final product. When selecting a ghostwriter, look for someone who understands your vision, has experience in your industry or topic area, and has a proven track record of success.

5. Establish clear communication and collaboration processes with your ghostwriter. A successful collaboration requires open, honest, and regular communication. Set expectations upfront, create a timeline and milestones, and schedule regular check-ins to ensure your book stays on track and aligns with your vision.

6. Leverage the power of AI-assisted writing to streamline the process and enhance your book's quality. By working with a ghostwriter who understands and utilizes the latest AI writing tools, you can benefit from increased efficiency, content optimization, and data-driven insights to create a truly standout book.

If you're looking for a skilled, experienced, and AI-savvy ghostwriter to help you bring your book idea to life, look no further. Our team of professional ghostwriters specializes in working with business leaders, entrepreneurs, and experts to create high-impact, authority-building books that drive real results.

By partnering with us, you'll benefit from:

- Our deep understanding of your industry and target audience, ensuring your book resonates and provides genuine value to your readers.
- Our proven track record of success in writing and publishing bestselling books for business growth and personal impact.

- Our seamless integration of cutting-edge AI writing tools to enhance the quality, efficiency, and data-driven insights of your book.
- Our commitment to open, collaborative communication and a customized approach tailored to your unique needs and goals.

We understand that writing a book is a deeply personal and transformative journey, and we're here to support you every step of the way. From initial ideation and planning to final editing and publication, our team will work tirelessly to ensure your book exceeds your expectations and achieves your desired impact.

So, if you're ready to take the next step in your book-writing journey and create a legacy that lasts, we invite you to schedule a free consultation with our team. During this call, we'll take the time to understand your vision, answer any questions you may have, and explore how we can best support you in bringing your book to life.

Don't let your message go unheard, or your impact unrealized. The time to act is now. Your book has the power to change lives, transform businesses, and shape the future of your industry. Let us help you make it a reality.

To schedule your free consultation and take the first step towards your book-writing dreams, visit [insert website or booking link] or contact us directly at [insert email or phone number].

We can't wait to hear from you and support you on this incredible journey. Together, let's unleash the power of your book and create a legacy that lasts.

Getting Started on Your Book Journey

Now that you've gained a deep understanding of the transformative power of a book for your business, and the steps involved in bringing your book to life, it's time to take action and embark on your own book-writing journey. Getting started can feel overwhelming, but by breaking the process down into manageable steps and utilizing the right resources and tools, you'll be well on your way to crafting a compelling and impactful book.

Specific Guidance on the First Steps to Begin Creating a Book

To help you kick-start your book-writing process, here's a checklist of initial actions you can take:

1. Clarify your book's purpose and core message. Ask yourself why you want to write this book, what value it will provide to your readers, and how it aligns with your business goals.
2. Identify your target audience. Understand who your ideal reader is, what challenges they face, and how your book will address their needs and aspirations.
3. Brainstorm and organize your book ideas. Use mind mapping, outlining, or other brainstorming techniques to gather your thoughts and start structuring your book's content.
4. Set realistic goals and create a writing schedule. Determine how much time you can dedicate to writing each week and establish a regular writing routine to keep yourself accountable.
5. Create a supportive writing environment. Designate a quiet, distraction-free space for writing and gather any necessary tools or resources, such as a computer, notebook, or reference materials.

When setting goals and timelines for your book project, it's essential to be realistic and allow for flexibility. Break your book-writing process down into smaller, achievable milestones, such as completing a chapter or section by a specific date. Celebrate each milestone along the way to maintain momentum and motivation.

Remember, writing a book is a marathon, not a sprint. Be patient with yourself and trust in the process. Consistency and perseverance are key to making steady progress and bringing your book to fruition.

Resources and Tools to Overcome Challenges and Obstacles

As you embark on your book-writing journey, you may encounter various challenges and obstacles, such as writer's block, self-doubt, or difficulty staying organized and focused. Here are some strategies, resources, and tools to help you overcome these common hurdles:

1. Embrace freewriting and stream-of-consciousness techniques. When faced with writer's block, try writing continuously for a set period without editing or censoring yourself. This can help unlock new ideas and insights.
2. Use writing prompts and exercises to stimulate creativity. Explore online resources like The Write Practice (thewritepractice.com) or Writing Exercises (writingexercises.co.uk) for a variety of prompts and exercises to get your creative juices flowing.
3. Break your writing sessions into smaller, focused blocks. Use the Pomodoro Technique or similar time-management strategies to maintain focus and avoid burnout. Apps like Forest (forestapp.cc) or Tomato Timer (tomato-timer.com) can be helpful for structuring your writing sessions.
4. Cultivate a growth mindset and practice self-compassion. Recognize that setbacks and challenges are a normal part of the writing process. Treat yourself with kindness and view obstacles as opportunities for learning and growth.
5. Join a writing community or find an accountability partner. Connect with fellow business authors through online communities like Scribophile (scribophile.com), or The Write Life (thewritelife.com) for support, feedback, and encouragement.
6. Experiment with different writing software and tools. Explore apps like Scrivener, Ulysses, or iA Writer to find a writing environment that suits your needs and preferences. Consider using mind mapping software like MindMeister (mindmeister.com) or XMind (xmind.net) to organize your ideas and structure your book's content.

By implementing these strategies and utilizing the right resources and tools, you'll be better equipped to navigate the challenges of the writing process and make steady progress on your book project. Remember, every author faces obstacles along the way—what sets successful authors apart is their willingness to persevere, adapt, and keep moving forward.

As you take these first steps on your book-writing journey, trust in your unique voice, expertise, and the value of your message. Your book has the power to transform lives, businesses, and industries. Embrace the journey ahead, stay committed to your vision, and know that with each word you write, you're one step closer to unleashing the full potential of your book and making a lasting impact on the world.

Recommended Resources and Tools for Aspiring Business Authors

While our ghostwriting services provide a comprehensive solution for bringing your book to life, we understand that some authors may prefer to tackle the writing process independently or seek additional support and resources along the way. To help you navigate your book-writing journey with confidence and ease, we've compiled a list of recommended online tools, books, and courses that can provide valuable guidance and inspiration.

Online Tools for Planning, Writing, and Promoting Your Book

1. Scrivener (literatureandlatte.com): A powerful writing software that helps you organize your ideas, structure your content, and manage your writing projects from start to finish.
2. Grammarly (grammarly.com): An AI-powered writing assistant that helps you polish your prose, catch errors, and improve your writing style for clarity and impact.
3. Publisher Rocket (publisherrocket.com): A comprehensive book marketing tool that helps you optimize your book's

metadata, research keywords, and gain valuable insights into your target market.

4. Canva (canva.com): A user-friendly graphic design platform that allows you to create professional-looking book covers, social media graphics, and promotional materials with ease.

Books on Writing, Publishing, and Marketing Your Book

1. "Bird by Bird" by Anne Lamott: A classic guide on the writing process, offering wisdom, humor, and practical advice for overcoming obstacles and finding your voice as a writer.

2. "On Writing Well" by William Zinsser: An essential resource for nonfiction writers, providing clear, concise guidance on crafting engaging and effective prose.

3. "The Business of Being a Writer" by Jane Friedman: A comprehensive guide to the business side of writing, covering topics such as market research, branding, and income diversification.

4. "Perennial Seller" by Ryan Holiday: A deep dive into the art of creating and marketing products that stand the test of time, including books that make a lasting impact.

Online Courses and Communities for Business Authors

1. Self Publishing School (self-publishingschool.com): A comprehensive online course that guides you through the entire process of writing, publishing, and marketing your book, with a focus on strategies for business growth.

2. Authority Pub Academy (authoritypub.com): A training program and community for entrepreneurs and professionals who want to establish their authority and grow their business through writing and publishing.

3. The Writer's Circle (thewriterscircle.net): An online community of writers, offering courses, workshops, and support groups to help you hone your craft and connect with fellow authors.

These resources offer a wealth of knowledge, tools, and support to help you write, publish, and promote your book effectively. Whether you're looking to improve your writing skills, streamline your book-writing process, or develop a powerful marketing strategy, these recommendations can provide the guidance and inspiration you need to succeed.

However, it's important to remember that the most valuable resource in your book-writing journey is your own unique perspective, expertise, and voice. No tool or course can replace the power of your authentic message, and the impact it can have on your readers and your business.

As you explore these resources and embark on your book-writing journey, remember to stay true to your vision, trust in the value of your ideas, and don't be afraid to seek support and guidance when you need it. Whether you choose to work with a ghostwriter or tackle the writing process on your own, the key is to stay committed to your goals and to keep moving forward, one word at a time.

By combining your own unique insights with the knowledge and tools available through these recommended resources, you'll be well-equipped to write a book that not only grows your business but also leaves a lasting impact on your readers and your industry. So, dive in, explore these resources, and most importantly, start writing —your book is waiting to be born!

Joining the Community of Business Authors

As you embark on your book-writing journey, it's important to remember that you're not alone. You are joining a vibrant and growing community of entrepreneurs, professionals, and thought leaders who have recognized the transformative power of books for business growth and personal impact.

By becoming a part of this movement, you have the opportunity to connect with like-minded individuals who share your passion for leveraging books to make a difference. Engaging with this community can provide you with invaluable support, inspiration, and opportunities for growth and collaboration.

Connecting with and Supporting Fellow Business Authors

One of the most powerful aspects of being a part of the business author community is the potential for mutual support and encouragement. As you navigate the challenges and triumphs of writing and promoting your book, having a network of fellow authors to lean on can make all the difference.

We encourage you to actively seek out and connect with other business authors in your network and beyond. Attend industry events, join online forums and social media groups, and participate in book-related discussions and initiatives. By engaging with your fellow authors, you can share your experiences, learn from their insights, and offer your own guidance and support in return.

Consider reaching out to authors whose books have resonated with you or whose expertise aligns with your own. Express your appreciation for their work and explore opportunities for connection and collaboration. Remember, building genuine relationships based on mutual respect and shared values is key to fostering a strong and supportive community.

Collaboration, Cross-Promotion, and Knowledge-Sharing Opportunities

Being a part of the business author community opens up a world of opportunities for collaboration, cross-promotion, and knowledge-sharing. By partnering with fellow authors, you can amplify your message, reach new audiences, and create mutually beneficial relationships that support your business goals.

Some potential collaboration and cross-promotion opportunities include:

1. Co-authoring a book or series: Partnering with another expert in your field to create a joint publication that combines your unique perspectives and expertise.

2. Participating in joint book launches or promotional campaigns: Coordinating with fellow authors to cross-promote your books, share each other's content, and leverage your combined networks for greater impact.
3. Hosting or participating in webinars, workshops, or events: Collaborating with other authors to deliver valuable content, share knowledge, and engage with your target audience in interactive formats.
4. Contributing to each other's blogs, podcasts, or other content platforms: Sharing your insights and expertise as a guest contributor on fellow authors' platforms, and inviting them to do the same on yours.
5. Forming mastermind groups or accountability partnerships: Joining forces with a small group of dedicated authors to provide ongoing support, feedback, and accountability as you work towards your book-writing and business goals.

By actively seeking out and embracing these opportunities for collaboration and knowledge-sharing, you can tap into the collective wisdom and resources of the business author community and accelerate your own growth and success.

A Movement for Change and Impact

Beyond the personal benefits of being a part of this community, joining the ranks of business authors means contributing to a larger movement for positive change and impact. As more entrepreneurs and professionals recognize the power of books to transform lives and industries, the collective influence of this community grows stronger.

By adding your voice and expertise to this movement, you are helping to shape the future of business, leadership, and innovation. Your book has the potential to inspire, educate, and empower countless readers, creating a ripple effect of positive change that extends far beyond your own network.

As you continue on your book-writing journey, remember that you are part of something greater than yourself. Embrace the support, opportunities, and collective wisdom of the business author community, and let it fuel your motivation and commitment to making a lasting impact through your work.

Together, as a community of passionate, purpose-driven authors, we have the power to redefine what it means to be a successful business leader and to create a brighter, more impactful future for us all. So, step into your role as a change-maker, connect with your fellow authors, and let's write the next chapter of business growth and transformation together.

Closing Thoughts...Gratitude

As we conclude this journey through the pages of *Take the Book by the Horns: Grow your business—as a published expert!* I want to take a moment to express my deepest gratitude for your time, trust, and commitment to your book-writing journey.

By investing in yourself and your business through the act of writing a book, you are taking a bold and transformative step towards unlocking your full potential and making a lasting impact on the world. Your dedication to this path is a testament to your vision, courage, and belief in the power of your ideas and expertise.

Throughout this book, we've explored the many ways in which a book can revolutionize your business, establish your authority, and open doors to incredible opportunities. We've delved into the challenges and rewards of the writing process, and provided practical strategies and tools to help you bring your book to life with clarity, impact, and authenticity.

As you embark on this transformative journey, know that you are not alone. You are joining a vibrant community of entrepreneurs, thought leaders, and change-makers who have harnessed the power of books to shape their industries and leave a lasting legacy. Embrace the support, wisdom, and inspiration of this community, and let it fuel your own journey towards success and significance.

Remember, your book has the potential to change lives, transform businesses, and reshape the future of your field. Your unique perspective, hard-earned insights, and passionate voice are needed now more than ever. By sharing your message through the pages of your book, you are not only investing in your own growth and success but also contributing to the collective wisdom and progress of your industry and the world at large.

As you take the next steps on your book-writing journey, trust in the process, stay committed to your vision, and embrace the challenges as opportunities for growth and discovery. The path may not always be easy, but the rewards—both personal and professional—are truly immeasurable.

If at any point along the way you find yourself in need of expert assistance, know that our team at Ghostwriter Marketing is here to help. Our services are designed to help busy entrepreneurs and professionals like you bring your book to life with ease, impact, and authenticity.

With our AI-powered tools and experienced team of writers, editors, and strategists, we can help you navigate every stage of the book-writing process—from ideation and planning to writing, editing, and promotion. Our proven process and track record of success have helped countless authors transform their ideas into powerful, impactful books that drive business growth and establish their authority in their field.

If you're ready to take your book-writing journey to the next level and create a book that truly stands out, we invite you to book a free consultation with our team. During this no-obligation call, we'll take the time to understand your unique goals, challenges, and vision for your book and explore how our services can support you in bringing your message to life.

To learn more about our ghostwriting services, and book your free consultation, visit GhostwriterMarketing.com. We're here to help you every step of the way and can't wait to see the incredible impact your book will make.

As I close this book, I want to leave you with a final reminder of the incredible potential that lies ahead of you. Your book is not just a project, or a goal—it's a powerful tool for transformation, growth, and impact. It's a key that can unlock doors to new opportunities, relationships, and levels of success you never thought possible.

So, take a deep breath, trust in yourself and your message, and take that first step towards making your book a reality. The world is waiting for your voice and your vision. It's time to share it with courage, confidence, and conviction.

Thank you again for joining me on this journey through the pages of *Take the Book by the Horns*. It has been an honor to share these insights and strategies with you, and I am truly excited to see the incredible books and businesses that will emerge as a result.

Here's to your success, your impact, and the incredible journey ahead.

With gratitude,

Lance Haverkamp
and the Staff at Ghostwriter Marketing